FLOYD CLYMER'S MOTORCYCLIST'S LIBRARY

The Book of the
B.S.A.

A COMPLETE GUIDE FOR OWNERS OF B.S.A.
MOTOR-CYCLES (COVERS VEE-TWINS AND
SINGLE-CYLINDER MODELS FROM
1936 TO 1939)

BY

W. C. HAYCRAFT, F.R.S.A.

NINTH EDIT.
1939

ANNOUNCEMENT

By special arrangement with the original publishers of this book, Sir Isaac Pitman & Son, Ltd., of London, England, we have secured the exclusive publishing rights for this book, as well as all others in THE MOTORCYCLIST'S LIBRARY.

Included in THE MOTORCYCLIST'S LIBRARY are complete instruction manuals covering the care and operation of respective motorcycles and engines; valuable data on speed tuning, and thrilling accounts of motorcycle race events. See listing of available titles elsewhere in this edition.

We consider it a privilege to be able to offer so many fine titles to our customers.

FLOYD CLYMER
Publisher of Books Pertaining to Automobiles and Motorcycles
2125 W. PICO ST.   LOS ANGELES 6, CALIF.

INTRODUCTION

Welcome to the world of digital publishing ~ the book you now hold in your hand, while unchanged from the original edition, was printed using the latest state of the art digital technology. The advent of print-on-demand has forever changed the publishing process, never has information been so accessible and it is our hope that this book serves your informational needs for years to come. If this is your first exposure to digital publishing, we hope that you are pleased with the results. Many more titles of interest to the classic automobile and motorcycle enthusiast, collector and restorer are available via our website at www.VelocePress.com. We hope that you find this title as interesting as we do.

NOTE FROM THE PUBLISHER

The information presented is true and complete to the best of our knowledge. All recommendations are made without any guarantees on the part of the author or the publisher, who also disclaim all liability incurred with the use of this information.

TRADEMARKS

We recognize that some words, model names and designations, for example, mentioned herein are the property of the trademark holder. We use them for identification purposes only. This is not an official publication.

INFORMATION ON THE USE OF THIS PUBLICATION

This manual is an invaluable resource for the classic motorcycle enthusiast and a "must have" for owners interested in performing their own maintenance. However, in today's information age we are constantly subject to changes in common practice, new technology, availability of improved materials and increased awareness of chemical toxicity. As such, it is advised that the user consult with an experienced professional prior to undertaking any procedure described herein. While every care has been taken to ensure correctness of information, it is obviously not possible to guarantee complete freedom from errors or omissions or to accept liability arising from such errors or omissions. Therefore, any individual that uses the information contained within, or elects to perform or participate in do-it-yourself repairs or modifications acknowledges that there is a risk factor involved and that the publisher or its associates cannot be held responsible for personal injury or property damage resulting from the use of the information or the outcome of such procedures.

WARNING!

One final word of advice, this publication is intended to be used as a reference guide, and when in doubt the reader should consult with a qualified technician.

CHAPTER I

ALL ABOUT CARBURATION

ALL B.S.A. models are sent out from the works with the carburettors carefully tuned and with jet sizes giving the best all-round performance. In the ordinary way it is not wise to alter the maker's setting, but sometimes it is necessary to retune the carburettor when, for instance, the original setting has been interfered with or the rider wishes to indulge in racing. In this chapter the author has given full information and tuning instructions for the three types of Amal carburettors fitted to the B.S.A. range. These carburettors comprise the semi-automatic two-lever needle jet carburettor fitted to most B.S.A.'s, the road racing T.T. carburettor fitted to the "Gold Stars" (1938-9), and the single-lever instrument which will be found on some of the 250 c.c. models.

THE TWO-LEVER NEEDLE JET AMAL CARBURETTOR

This carburettor has been practically unchanged for many years, and the advice given hereafter applies to 1936 onwards. In order to tune the carburettor intelligently it is necessary to grasp how the instrument works.

How It Works. The carburettor fitted to all except certain 1939 and earlier 250 c.c. engines is of the two-lever needle jet type, the mixture at slow or idling speeds being controlled by a readily adjustable pilot jet, whilst at higher speeds the mixture is controlled by means of a needle attached to the throttle slide and working in a restriction jet. The two-lever control must not be confused with the type of control that was used a considerable time ago on the two-lever carburettor, in which it was necessary constantly to adjust the air lever in accordance with the conditions under which the machine was running. This carburettor is for all practical purposes automatic, the air lever being closed only to facilitate starting and occasionally under very adverse circumstances. The carburettor slides are chromium plated to provide hard wearing surfaces.

Referring to Fig. 1, showing a sectional view of the instrument, A is the carburettor body or mixing chamber, the upper part of which has a throttle valve B, with taper needle C attached by the needle clip. The throttle valve regulates the quantity of mixture supplied to the engine. Passing through the throttle valve is the air valve *D*, independently operated, and serving the purpose of obstructing the main air passage for starting and mixture

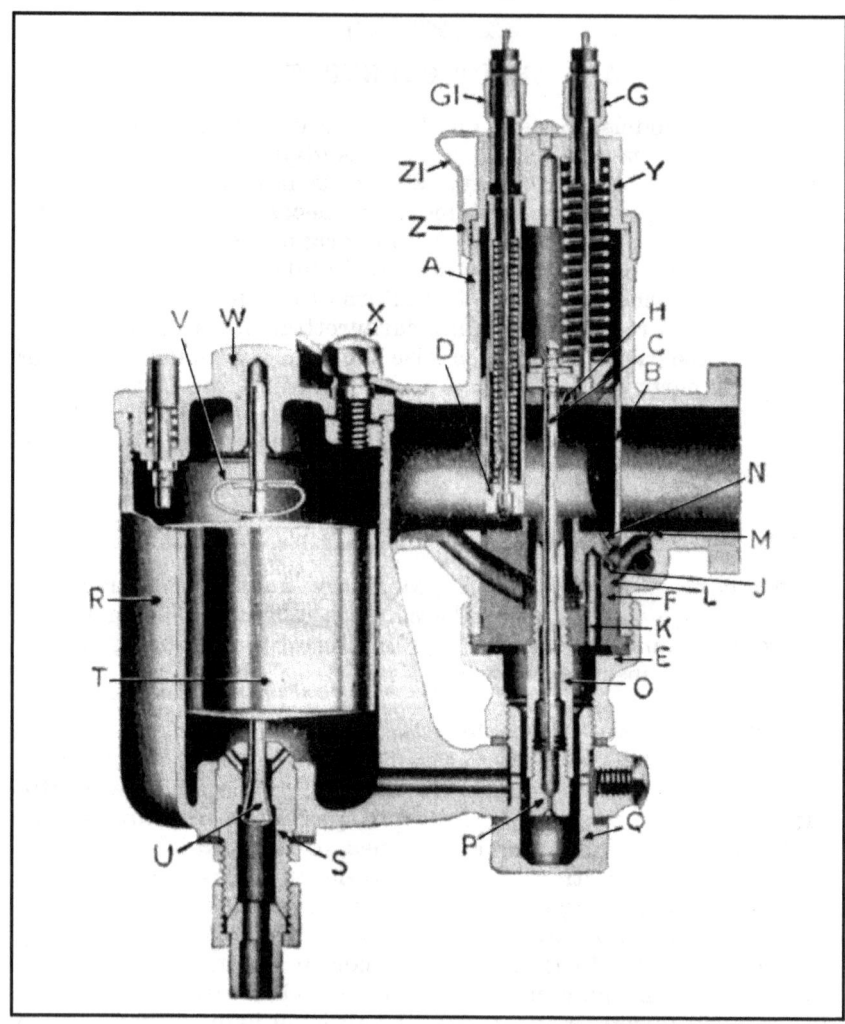

Fig. 1. Sectional View of Two-lever Needle-jet Amal Carburettor

regulation. On the upperside of the jet block is the adaptor body *H*, forming a clean through-way. Integral with the jet block is the pilot jet *J*, supplied through the passage *K*. The adjustable pilot air intake *L* communicates with a chamber, from which issues the pilot outlet *M* and the by-pass *N*. An adjusting screw (*TS*, Fig. 2) is provided on the mixing chamber, by which the position of the throttle valve for tick-over is regulated independently of the cable adjustment. The needle jet O is screwed in the underside of the jet block, and carries at its bottom end the main jet P. Both these jets are removable when the jet plug Q, which bolts the mixing chamber and the float chamber together, is removed. The float chamber, which has bottom feed, consists of a cup R supplied with petrol by union S. It contains the float T and the needle valve U attached by the clip V. The float chamber cover W has a lock screw X for security.

The petrol tap having been turned on, petrol will flow past the needle valve U until the quantity of petrol in the chamber R is sufficient to raise the float T, when the needle valve U will prevent a further supply from entering the float chamber until some in the chamber has already been used up by the engine. The float chamber having filled to its correct level, the fuel passes along the passages through the diagonal holes in the jet plug Q, when it will be in communication with the main jet P and the pilot feed hole K; the level in the needle jet and pilot jet is, obviously, the same as that maintained in the float chamber.

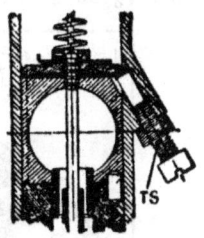

FIG. 2. AMAL THROTTLE STOP

Imagine the throttle valve B very slightly open. As the piston descends, a partial vacuum is created in the carburettor, causing a rush of air through the pilot air hole L, and drawing fuel from the pilot jet J. The mixture of air and fuel is admitted to the engine through the pilot outlet M. The quantity of mixture capable of being passed by the pilot outlet M is insufficient to run the engine. This mixture also carries excess of fuel. Consequently, before a combustible mixture is admitted, throttle valve B must be slightly raised, admitting a further supply of air from the main air intake. The further the throttle valve is opened, the less will be the depression on the outlet M, but, in turn, a higher depression will be created on the by-pass N, and the pilot mixture will flow from this passage as well as from the outlet M. The mixture supplied by the pilot and by-pass system is supplemented at about one-eighth throttle by fuel from the main jet P, the throttle valve cut-away determining the mixture strength from here to one-quarter throttle. Proceeding up the throttle range, mixture control by the needle position occurs from one-quarter to three-quarters throttle, and from this point the main jet is the only regulation.

The air valve D, which is cable-operated on the two-lever carburettor, has the effect of obstructing the main through-way and, in consequence, increasing the depression on the main jet, enriching the mixture. Two adjusters are provided on the handlebars for cable adjustment.

Tuning the Two-lever Carburettor.* Should the setting of this instrument not give entire satisfaction for particular requirements, there are four separate ways of rectifying matters as given herewith, and the adjustments should be made in this order: (*a*) Main jet (¾ to full throttle); (*b*) Pilot air adjustment (closed to ⅛ throttle); (*c*) Throttle valve cut-away on the air-intake side (⅛ to ¼ throttle); (*d*) Needle position (¼ to ¾ throttle). The

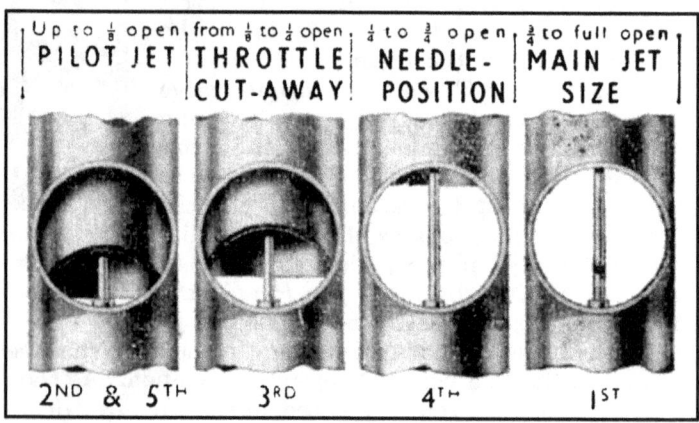

Fig. 3. Range and Sequence of Tuning—Amal Carburettor

diagram (Fig. 3) clearly indicates the part of the throttle range over which each adjustment is effective.

(*a*) To obtain the correct main jet size, several jets should be experimented with, and that selected should be the *smallest which gives maximum power and speed* on full throttle. But the size recommended by the manufacturer will usually be found to be the best.

(*b*) To weaken the slow-running mixture, screw the pilot air adjuster outwards, and to enrich the mixture screw the pilot air adjuster inwards.

Screw pilot air adjuster home in a clockwise direction. Place gear lever in "neutral." Slightly flood the float chamber by gently depressing the tickler until fuel begins to escape from the mixing chamber. Slightly retard the ignition, open the throttle about ¼ open, close the air lever, start the engine, and warm up. After warming up, reduce the engine revolutions by gently throttling

---

* These instructions apply also to the "pump" type carburettor fitted to the 1936 Models R20, Q21, Q8, R5. In this case a 15 per cent larger main jet is needed and the needle should be lowered one notch.

down. The slow-running mixture will prove over-rich unless air leaks exist. Very gradually unscrew the pilot jet adjuster. The engine speed will increase, and must again be reduced by gently closing the throttle until, by a combination of throttle positions and air adjustment, the desired "idling" is obtained. It is occasionally necessary to retard the "Magdyno" completely before getting a satisfactory tick-over, especially when early ignition timing

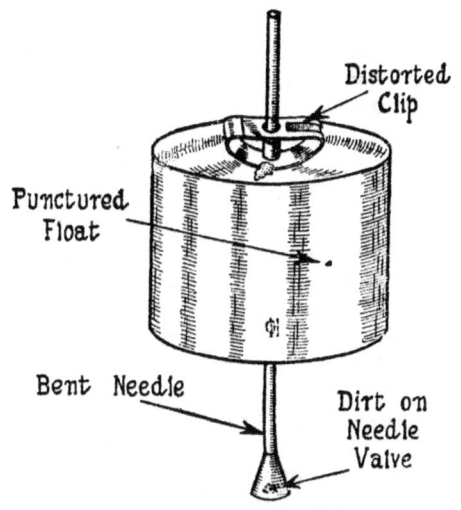

FIG. 4. SOME POSSIBLE CAUSES OF PERSISTENT FLOODING OF THE FLOAT CHAMBER

is used. If it is desired to make the engine idle with the throttle quite closed, the position of the throttle valve must be set by means of the throttle stop screw, the throttle twist-grip during this adjustment being rotated to the fully closed position. Alternatively, if the screw is adjusted clear of the throttle valve, the engine will be shut off in the normal way by the twist-grip. Do not take the throttle stop screw out completely.

(c) Given satisfactory "tick-over," set the ignition lever at half-advance and the air lever fully open. Very slowly open the throttle valve, when, if the engine responds regularly up to one-quarter throttle, the valve cut-away is correct.

A weak mixture is indicated by spitting-back through the air intake, with blue flames and hesitation in picking up, which disappears when the air lever is closed down. This can be remedied by fitting a throttle valve with less cut-away. A rich mixture is shown by a black sooty exhaust, and the engine falters when the air valve is closed. The remedy for this is a throttle valve with greater cut-away. Each Amal valve is stamped with two numbers, the first indicating the type number of the carburettor, and the second figure the amount of cut-away on the intake side of the valve in sixteenths of an inch, e.g. 6/4 is a type 6 valve with $\tfrac{4}{16}$ in. or a ¼ in. cut-away.

(d) Open air lever fully and the throttle half-way. Note if the exhaust is crisp and the engine flexible. Close the air valve slightly below the throttle, when the exhaust note and engine revolutions should remain constant. Should popping-back and spitting occur with blue flames from the intake, the mixture is weak, and the needle should be slightly raised. Test by lowering the air valve gently. The engine revolutions will rise when the air valve is lowered slightly below the throttle valve.

If the engine speed does not increase progressively with raising of the throttle, and a smoky exhaust is apparent, with heavy, laboured running, and tendency to eight-stroke, the mixture is too rich and the needle should be lowered in the throttle valve. Having found the correct needle position, the carburettor setting is now complete, and it will be found that the driving is practically automatic once the engine is warmed up. For speed work on petrol fuels the main jet may be increased by 10 per cent, when the air lever should be fully open on full throttle. If extreme economy is desired, lower the needle one groove farther after carrying out the four series of tests described above.

Possible Causes of Bad Slow-running. If it is found impossible to obtain good slow-running by making the pilot air adjustment as described in paragraph (b) on page 4, it is probable that some defect other than carburation is responsible for preventing the engine running slowly at low revolutions. Air leaks are a possible cause which should be looked for. They may be due to a poor joint at the carburettor attachment to the cylinder and/or a worn inlet valve guide. Badly seating valves will also weaken the mixture. Defects in the ignition system may also be responsible for poor tick-over. The sparking plug may be oily, or the points set too close (see page 56). Possibly the spark is excessively advanced or the contact-breaker needs attention (see page 57). Examine the slip ring for oil and see that the pick-up brush is bedding down and in good condition. Also examine the H.T. cable for signs of shorting.

1937 Type Air Cleaners. The air cleaner fitted to the Amal carburettor on many 1937 B.S.A.'s requires no maintenance attention other than removal and cleaning of the felt filter bag every 2000 miles. To clean the bag, pour petrol on the inside to wash away all impurities and then when dry brush sharply with a small stiff brush. Afterwards refit the filter on the carburettor. When driving in very dusty conditions or tropical climates it is wise to clean the filter bag about every 1000 miles, Maintenance of later air cleaners are dealt with on page 26.

For Racing. A genuine fifty-fifty petrol-benzole mixture is suitable used in conjunction with a high-compression piston, but for speed work an alcohol fuel such as R.D.I. gives perhaps the best results. Tune for speed and disregard fuel consumption. The main jet may be increased by about 10 per cent for speed work (much more for alcohol fuels).

Maintenance of the Amal Carburettor. Periodical cleaning is necessary to maintain efficient functioning of the carburettor, and should be carried out in the following sequence.

Disconnect petrol pipe. Unscrew the jet plug Q (Fig. 1) and remove float chamber complete. With box or set spanner, slacken the mixing chamber union nut E. Mixing chamber complete may now be removed by unscrewing set-bolts holding the carburettor on the induction flange. Unscrew mixing chamber lock ring Z (held by clip ZI), and pull out throttle valve, needle, and air valve. Remove main jet P and needle jet O. Mixing chamber union nut E may then be removed and jet block complete pushed out. If this is obstinate, tap gently, using a wooden stump inside the mixing chamber. Slacken lock screw X and unscrew float chamber cover W. Withdraw the float by pinching the clip V inwards, and at the same time pull gently upwards.

Generally it is sufficient to wash all the parts in clean petrol, but if the carburettor has had extended service, check the following—

(a) FLOAT CHAMBER NEEDLE U. If a distinct shoulder is visible on the point of seating, renew needle as soon as convenient. If no shoulder exists, but seating is not good, polish by rotating the needle with the fingers.

(b) THROTTLE VALVE. Test in mixing chamber, and if excessive play is present it is advisable to renew valve without delay.

(c) THROTTLE NEEDLE CLIP. This part must securely grip needle. *Free rotation must not take place*, otherwise the needle groove will become worn and necessitate a new part being fitted. *Be sure to refit the clip in the same groove.*

(d) JET BLOCK. If trouble has been experienced with erratic "idling," ascertain by means of a fine bristle that the pilot jet J is clear, and that the pilot outlet M in the mixing chamber is unobstructed.

To Reassemble. Refit jet block F with washer on underside and screw on lightly mixing chamber union nut E. Screw in needle jet O and main jet P. Open air lever $\frac{7}{8}$ in., throttle lever half-way; grasp the air slide between the thumb and the finger; *make sure that the needle enters the central hole in the adaptor top.* Slightly twist the throttle valve until it enters the adaptor guide, when on pushing down the valves the air valve should enter its guide. If not, slightly move mixing chamber cap Y, when the air valve will slide into place. Screw on mixing chamber ring-nut. *No brute force is necessary.*

Attach carburettor to the cylinder, pushing right home, and examine washer if flange fitting. Refit float and needle, holding the needle head against its seating by means of a pencil until float and the clip V are positioned.

Make absolutely sure that the clip enters the groove provided. Screw on the cover tightly and lock in position by means of the lock screw X. Fit the jet plug Q to the float chamber (one washer above and one below the lug). Screw holding plug into mixing chamber and lock securely. Clean petrol pipe and filter if fitted, and replace. It will be necessary to re-check the pilot setting if this has been disturbed.

THE SINGLE-LEVER CARBURETTOR

The single-lever needle jet carburettor fitted on earlier "two-fifties" is of the same type and identically similar to the two-lever needle jet carburettor (dealt with in preceding pages) except for the following. The air valve and corresponding details are removed from the carburettor and replaced by a plug screw which screws into the mixing chamber cap in place of the air lever cable adjuster. No strangling device is therefore included. Should difficult starting be experienced at any time, a rich starting mixture may always be obtained by use of the tickler on the float chamber cover.

From the foregoing it will be obvious that the tuning and maintenance instructions given on page 4 are applicable to the single-lever carburettor, except that all references to the air lever must be disregarded.

Position of Controls (All B.S.A.s). To ensure a quick start from cold, open the throttle twist-grip (inwards) about *one-eighth* of its total movement, close the air lever completely (when fitted) and retard the ignition lever slightly. The same control setting applies for a warm engine, but in this case the air lever should be opened slightly and the carburettor should not be flooded. Before attempting to start a new engine, remove the sparking plug and after placing the piston at the bottom of its stroke, pour about two teaspoonfuls of engine oil into the cylinder. As soon as the engine starts, advance the ignition fully, give full air and warm the engine up gradually.

THE AMAL T.T. CARBURETTOR

Special Features. Exceptional care has been taken in the design and manufacture of the choke which is based on a long racing experience. The choke offers the minimum resistance to the passage of the ingoing mixture from the carburettor, and so enables the engine to develop the utmost power and acceleration of which it is capable. Good acceleration is further ensured by the provision of means for adjusting the mixture strength at all throttle openings and the incorporation of an adjustable pilot jet which enables the engine to respond instantly to a sudden turn of the twist-grip. A special feature of the racing carburettor is the use of an external air valve at the side of the mixing chamber. This affords ample means of regulating the mixture strength without creating any obstruction to the main gas pressure, and it is thus possible to compensate for variations in atmospheric conditions and altitude.

Tuning the Racing Carburettor. Tuning the T.T. racing carburettor involves procedure very similar to that employed for the standard two-lever semi-automatic instrument, and the tuning sequence is the same. Make the adjustments in this order: (*a*) main jet; (*b*) pilot jet adjustment; (*c*) throttle valve cut-away; (*d*) needle position.

(*a*) To determine the size of the main jet, experiment with several jets and select the smallest jet which gives the *greatest maximum speed*. The air lever should be fully open during these tests on full throttle.

(*b*) Before attempting to set the pilot adjuster the engine should be run to its normal running temperature, otherwise a faulty adjustment is possible which will upset the correct selection of the throttle valve. The pilot adjuster which controls the amount of petrol passed is rotated clockwise to weaken the mixture, and anti-clockwise to richen the same. The pilot adjuster should be adjusted very gradually until a satisfactory tick-over is obtained, but care should be taken that the achievement of too slow a tick-over (i.e. slower than is actually necessary) does not lead to a "spot" which may cause stalling when the throttle is very slightly open.

(*c*) Having set the pilot adjuster the throttle should then be opened up progressively and positions noted where, if at all, the exhaust note becomes irregular. When this is noticed the throttle should be left open at this position and the air lever slightly closed, which will then give an indication as to whether the "spot" is a rich or a weak one.

If it is a rich "spot" a throttle valve should be fitted with more cut-away on the air intake side, and vice versa.

(*d*) The needle position will affect carburation up to somewhere over one-quarter throttle, after which the jet needle, which is suspended from the throttle valve, comes into action, and when the throttle is opened further and tests are again made for rich or weak spots, as previously outlined, the needle can be raised to enrich or lowered to weaken the mixture, whichever may be found necessary.

When the foregoing adjustments have been correctly made and the main jet size has been settled it will be found that a perfectly progressive mixture will be obtainable from tick-over to full throttle.

Alcohol Fuels. When alcohol fuel is used a needle jet size ·113 must be fitted, and it is also necessary to increase the main jet size by the following amounts—

P.M.S. 2 Fuel . 60 per cent greater flow than for petrol.
R.D.I. Fuel . 80 to 100 per cent greater flow than for petrol.

CHAPTER II
B.S.A. LUBRICATION

SINCE engine lubrication is the most vital, it will be dealt with before the lubrication of the cycle parts. Several types of B.S.A. lubrication systems have been used since 1935, but they may be grouped into dry and wet sump systems for convenience.

Five Points to Remember. Whatever type of lubrication system is provided, there are five essential points to observe. They are —
(1) A new engine must be run-in with great care.
(2) Sufficient oil must be kept in circulation.
(3) The oil must be of good quality.
(4) The oil must be kept clean.
(5) Oil dilution must not occur.

Until 1000-1500 Miles have been Covered. Large throttle openings should not be given and the engine should be nursed carefully, otherwise it may be *permanently* spoiled and never deliver its full power output. Bearing surfaces when new *appear* dead smooth, but actually are covered with fine tool marks (invisible to the naked eye), and until these disappear and a uniform mirror-like gloss and hardness spreads all over, local friction is very apt to occur and the oil film may break down at one or more places, aggravating matters still further. To speed on a new machine is a great temptation, but it must be resisted as it is definitely not "worth the candle." Many conscientious riders make a point of not exceeding 35 m.p.h. in top gear until running-in is completed, but the principal aim should be always to let the engine "run light," make full use of the gearbox and allow the engine *progressively* to do more work as the mileage mounts up. But never permit a sudden burst of full throttle. Half to three-quarter throttle is the maximum which should be allowed even during the last stages of running-in.

On dry sump lubricated engines with a gear-type pump (Fig. 5) used on all 1937 engines onwards no adjustment for the oil pump is provided (see page 14), but on 1936 singles and 1936-9 twin-cylinder 986 c.c. models with wet sump lubrication it is extremely important to make sure that the oil supply during the running-in period is adequate by setting the pump adjustment provided so that there is a continuous slight blue haze at the exhaust and an oil consumption of about 800-1000 m.p.g. Later on when the bearings have bedded down a better consumption may be obtained by cutting down the oil supply. In the case of machines with dry sump lubrication make sure that there is always plenty of oil in the tank (see page 16) or oil sump in the case of 1936 "Empire Star" models.

Use of Upper Cylinder Lubricant. The makers of the B.S.A. recommend the use of some upper cylinder lubricant during the first 1500 miles. Good lubricants are Mixtrol and Wakefield's

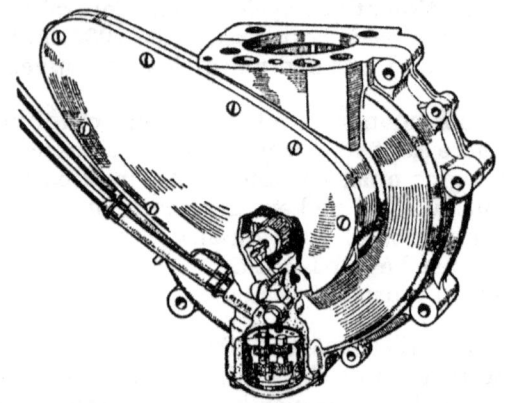

FIG. 5. ALL 1937-9 B.S.A. SINGLES WITH DRY SUMP LUBRICATION HAVE A GEAR TYPE OIL PUMP FITTED AS SHOWN
To remove the pump, detach the plate under the crankcase on timing side, and remove the pins holding pump in position

Castrollo, which should be mixed with the fuel, not the engine oil. As regards the proportion to use, follow the instructions issued by the makers of these proprietary lubricants.

Suitable Oils for B.S.A. Engines. If you would get the utmost performance and life from your B.S.A. engine, you should regularly replenish the oil tank or sump with one of the following oils recommended by the makers—

(1) Castrol Grand Prix (XL, winter).
(2) Golden Shell (Double Shell, winter). See also page 32.
(3) Mobiloil D (Mobiloil A, winter).
(4) Price's Energol SAE 60 (SAE 30, winter).
(5) Essoluble 60 (Essoluble 30, winter).

For racing purposes Castrol R is excellent, but it should be particularly noted that this is a vegetable oil and must *not* be mixed with any of the five mineral base oils mentioned above. If it is used in place of a mineral oil, first clean the oil tank.

For extra heavy duties (during the summer) it is permissible to use Essolube Racer instead of the above corresponding grade (Essolube 60).

DRY SUMP LUBRICATION

Four distinct designs of dry sump lubrication systems have been employed on 1936-9 B.S.A. engines, and the author will therefore deal with these types separately, giving first a brief outline of the method of oil distribution and then full maintenance instructions.

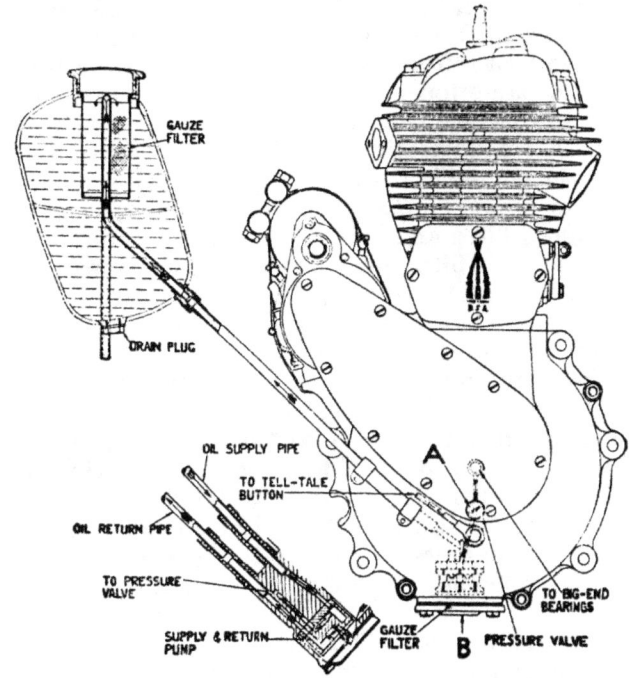

FIG. 6. DRY SUMP LUBRICATION SYSTEM (TYPE A)
Above is shown the arrangement on S.V. engines (see below)

The latest types will be dealt with first and for convenience the systems will be referred to as types A, B, C, D.

Type A (All 1937-9 Singles). All S.V. and O.H.V. single-cylinder engines have a lubrication system of the same design except, of course, that in the case of the O.H.V. engines provision is made for lubrication of the overhead valve gear. The "heart" of the dry sump system, as already mentioned, consists of a twin gear-type pump (Fig. 5) driven off the timing side main shaft and situated at the base of the crankcase on the right-hand side. All oil-ways are internal except, of course, the supply and return pipes leading from and to the oil tank. Fig. 6 illustrates the lubrication system used on all 350, 500, 600 c.c. B.S.A. side-valve engines. The arrangement on the 250 c.c. engines is identical except that there is no tell-tale provided (omitted also on some larger engines) and the oil tank and petrol tank are combined.

The oil flows from the oil tank along the supply pipe to the supply pump and is then force-fed past a pressure valve A (Figs. 6, 8) to the big-end bearing, details of which are shown in Fig. 7. On some 500, 600 c.c. S.V. and O.H.V. engines, however, some of the oil is by-passed from a point between the gear pump and the pressure valve to a tell-tale button mounted on the timing cover or petrol tank panel (on most models). The button should project about ¼ in. when the engine is running and the oil is in circulation. After lubricating the big-end bearing and circulating throughout the engine in the form of oil mist, all surplus oil drains to the bottom of the crankcase and is sucked up by the return pump through a filter and forced back into the oil tank through a second fine mesh filter provided inside the tank itself. Also contained within the tank is a pressure release valve.

On the O.H.V. engines some of the oil returning to the tank is by-passed up into the rocker-box through an external pipe connected by a union to the return pipe between the oil tank and return pump. After lubricating the two rocker spindles, valve guides, etc., surplus oil drains to the crankcase down another pipe connected to the base of the inlet valve spring housing at the side of the rocker-box. This may be clearly understood by reference to Fig. 8. In the case of the 1939 250 c.c. Model C11, however, there is no pressure feed for the rocker-box, oil mist from the crankcase sufficing. The pump is non-adjustable.

Type A—Maintenance. Where no oil indicator is provided, the oil circulation should be checked frequently by removing the oil tank filler cap while the engine is running and noting whether oil is being steadily ejected from the orifice of the return pipe. Where an indicator is fitted, keep an eye on the button and, if it fails to protrude about ¼ in., check up on the oil level in the tank. Partial failure of the oil supply and tell-tale (where fitted) is sometimes caused through some foreign matter getting on to the spring-loaded ball in the pressure valve, and the remedy is to remove screw A (Figs. 6, 8) and withdraw the ball and spring and clean the ball and its seating.

It should be noted that imperfect seating of the spring-loaded ball is liable to cause oil to flow from the tank to the engine while the engine is *stationary*. To avoid this nuisance clean both the ball and its seating thoroughly, replace the ball and deal it a sharp blow with a light hammer to ensure that it is bedding perfectly on its seating. Finally replace the spring and retaining screw.

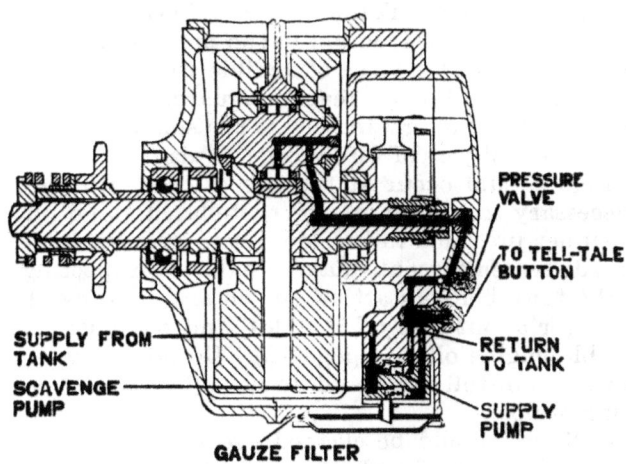

Fig. 7. Showing the Force Feed to the Big-end Bearing
The drawing shows a 1938 engine but applies also to 1937 and 1939 engines

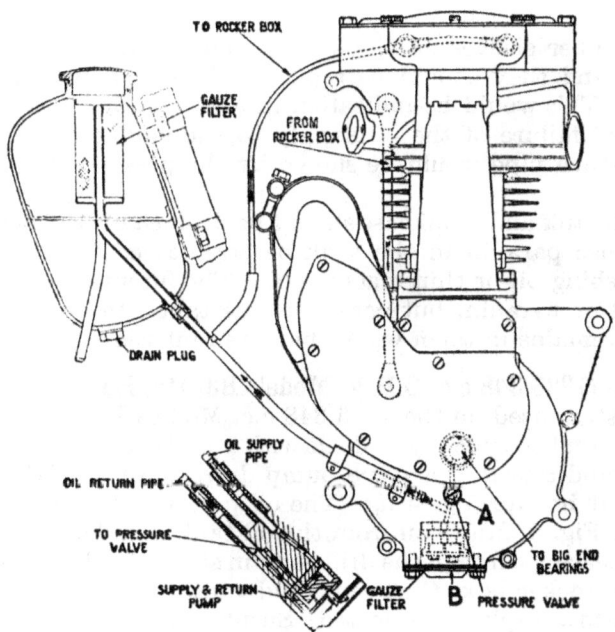

Fig. 8. Dry Sump Lubrication System (Type A)
Above is shown the arrangement on 1937-9 O.H.V. engines

Oil leakage at the oil tank filler cap may be occasioned by a rise in pressure due to an obstruction in the pressure release pipe and the remedy is to insert a piece of flexible wire into the lower end of the pipe (just ahead of the rear mudguard) and push it up until the wire protrudes through and clears the small orifice.

While on the subject of oil leakage it may be mentioned that if oil leakage should occur at the top of the push-rod casing, it is only necessary to tighten up the castellated gland nut with the special spanner provided in the tool kit to prevent it.

As regards replenishment, make a habit of inspecting the level of oil in the tank before starting out on any journey of considerable length (or about every 250 miles) and replenish if necessary with suitable engine oil (see page 12). Do not allow the level to fall below the half-full mark and do not fill above the level of the return pipe orifice.

The two filters should be cleaned every 2000 miles, the pump filter being withdrawn for the purpose by the removal of cover plate *B*, shown in Fig. 8. (*Note.* The pump is independently mounted and should not be disturbed.)

To remove the filter in the oil tank, unscrew the filler cap, and lift the filter out. (*Note.* When refilling with oil do not remove the filter.)

The rubber sleeves on the supply and return pipes should be oil-tight and they should be replaced if they show any signs of leakage. This would be indicated, in the case of the supply pipe, by partial failure of the oil supply to the engine, while leakage at the return pipe would be shown by the presence of oil at this point.

The oil tank and crankcase should be drained every 2000 miles.* Do not use paraffin in the tank or crankcase, but if necessary use a flushing oil or thin machine oil. The filters may be washed in petrol or paraffin, but care must be taken to ensure that no paraffin remains in them when they are replaced.

Type B (1936 348 c.c. O.H.V. Models B3, D5, R4, R19). The dry sump system used on the 1936 348 c.c. Models R4, R19, is somewhat different to type A just dealt with but also includes a separate oil tank and a twin gear-type pump driven from the timing side main shaft by worm gearing. The oil pump, details of which are shown in Fig. 9, draws oil from the oil tank and delivers it to the big-end bearing through the drilled main shaft, flywheel and crankpin. The rocker-box, push-rods, and cams are also pressure-fed. Other parts are splash-lubricated. Surplus oil drains to the base of the crankcase, is picked up by the rotating flywheels, and collected in a reservoir by a scraper on the flywheel rims. The oil is then

---

* This should be done immediately after a run when the oil is hot.

pumped by the scavenge pump from the reservoir back into the oil tank. As may be seen in Fig. 10, an external pipe is provided for rocker-box lubrication. An oil tell-tale is fitted on the timing cover.

Type B—Maintenance. An adjustment is provided for the pump. Top up the oil tank about every 250 miles with suitable

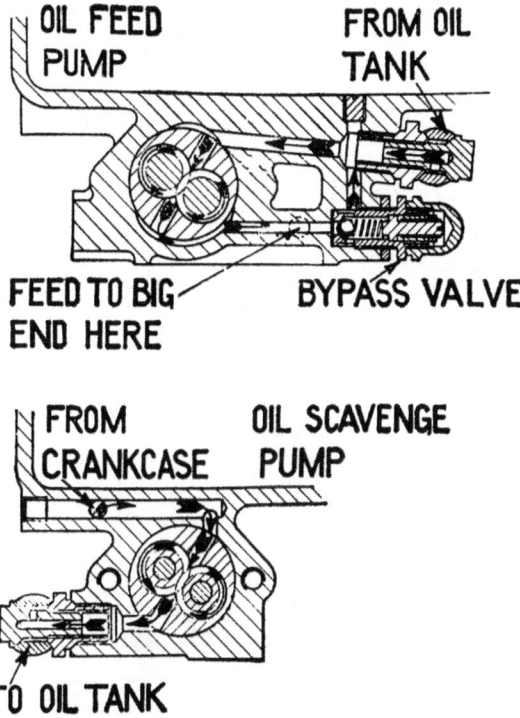

Fig. 9. Oil Pump Arrangement on 1936 Models B3, R4, R19

engine oil (page 12) but do not allow the oil level to rise above the return pipe orifice or to fall below the half-full mark. Oil circulation may be checked by means of the tell-tale button, the knob of which should protrude about ¼ in. when the engine is running. If the indicator fails to operate, examine the lubrication system after first checking that there is adequate oil in the tank. Occasionally wipe the stem of the indicator with a clean rag to ensure freedom of movement. With oil circulation correct, there should be a puff of blue smoke visible at the exhaust when suddenly accelerating. Adjust the pump if necessary.

About every 2000 miles drain both the oil tank and crankcase

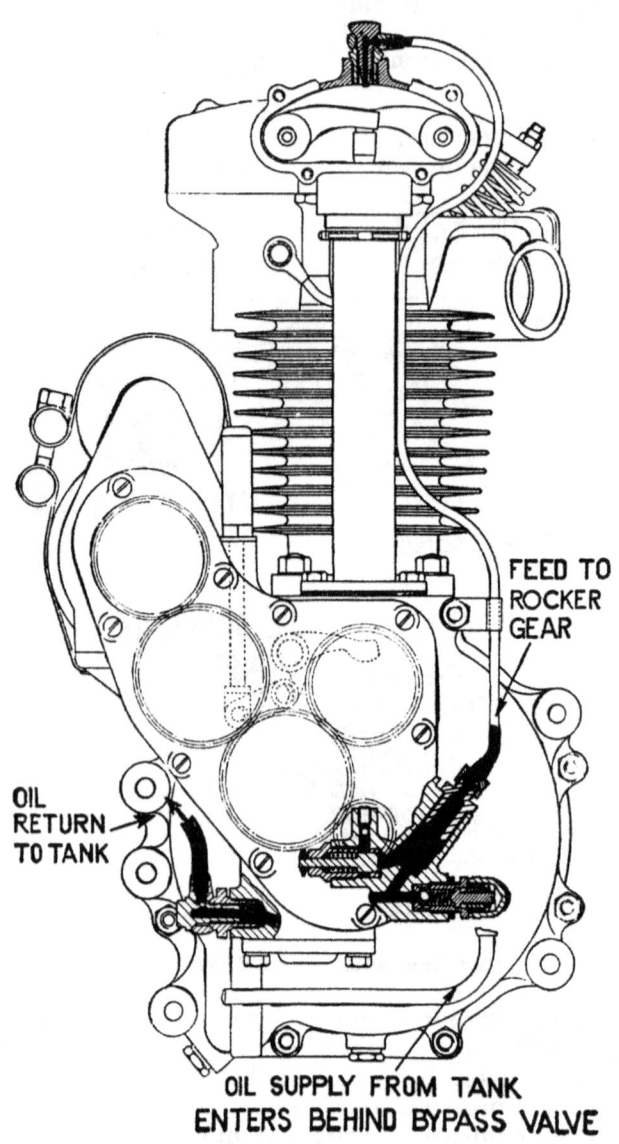

Fig. 10. Dry Sump Lubrication System (Type B)
This system is fitted only on the 1936 Models B3, R4, R19

when the oil is warm, flush out with flushing oil, unscrew and clean the oil tank filter and replenish the tank. Before starting up again put a little oil into the cylinder (see page 12) and nurse the engine for a few miles afterwards.

Type C (1936 Singles With "Sump" Oil Reservoirs). This system of lubrication used on eight 1936 singles (348, 499, 595 c.c.),

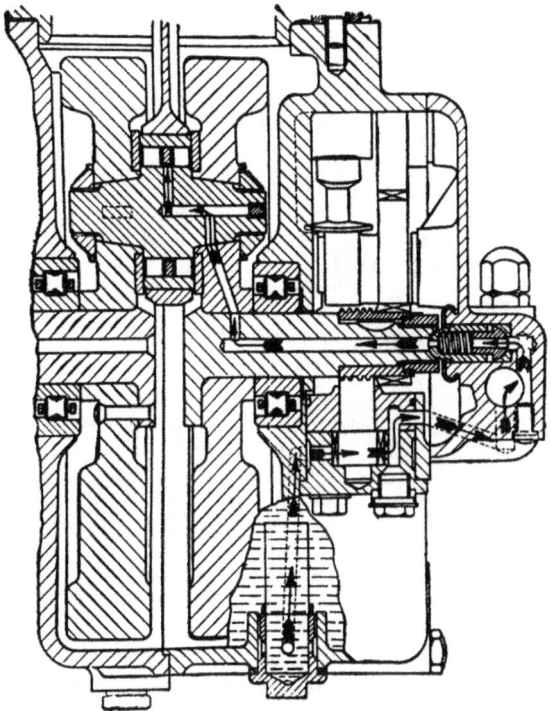

Fig. 11. Details of Oil Feed to Big-end Bearing
The arrangement shown applies to 1936 S.V. and O.H.V. engines with "sump" type oil reservoirs

while having features common to the type B system, differs mainly in that the oil reservoir is integral with the crankcase. A gear-type pump driven from the timing side main shaft by skew gearing draws filtered oil from the reservoir or "sump" and forces it to the big-end bearing through the drilled main shaft, flywheel, and crankpin. As in the case of the type B system, other parts are splash-lubricated and surplus oil draining to the bottom of the crankcase is picked up by the action of a scraper on the flywheel rims and returned to the "sump." With this system there are, of course, no external pipes whatever. Details of the oil feed to the big-end bearing are shown in Fig. 11, and Fig. 12 shows the general arrangement of the lubrication system. An oil pressure gauge mounted on the tank panel indicates oil pressure in pounds per square inch. On O.H.V. engines there is no automatic feed for the overhead valve gear (except the inlet valve guide), grease nipples being provided for the O.H. rockers. The oil supply is adjustable.

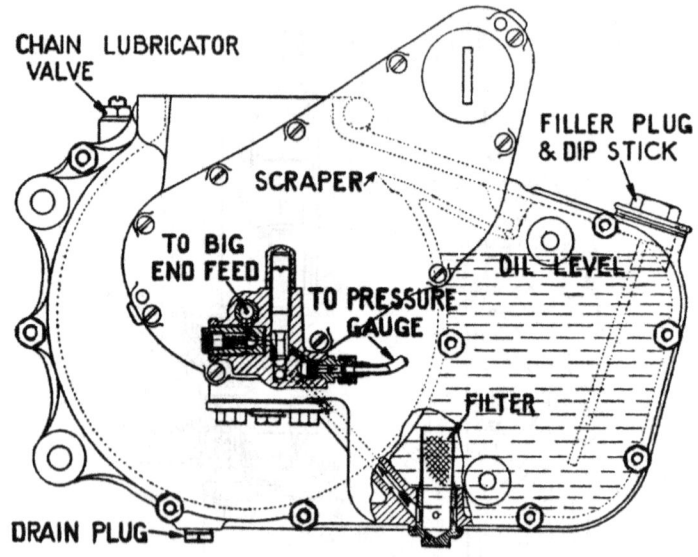

FIG. 12. DRY SUMP LUBRICATION SYSTEM (TYPE C)
This system applies to eight 1936 models (see text)

Type C—Maintenance. Top up the "sump" about every 250 miles with suitable engine oil (page 12). Attached to the filler cap plug is a dipstick with notches marked "1" and "2," the numbers indicating the quantity of oil in pints required to be added to the "sump" in order to fill it. B.S.A. owners should note that it is of extreme importance not to run a machine more than about 50 miles after the oil level has fallen to the "2" mark.

The normal reading for the pressure gauge is 5-12 lb. per sq. in., but these figures are quite arbitrary and it is advisable to judge if lubrication is correct by the running of the engine and the state of the exhaust rather than by the indicated pressure. On accelerating suddenly from a low speed a puff of blue smoke should leave the exhaust pipe. However, if the oil pressure declines appreciably, at once check over the lubrication system, after first examining the oil level in the "sump." Adjust the pump if necessary.

The crankcase and "sump" should be drained and flushed out with flushing oil and the filter cleaned with petrol about every 2000 miles. Drain while the oil is warm and before restarting put some oil in the cylinder (see page 12). Afterwards drive carefully for 50 miles. Every 250 miles the push-rod upper ends should be lubricated with an oil-can and the overhead rockers greased with a grease-gun.

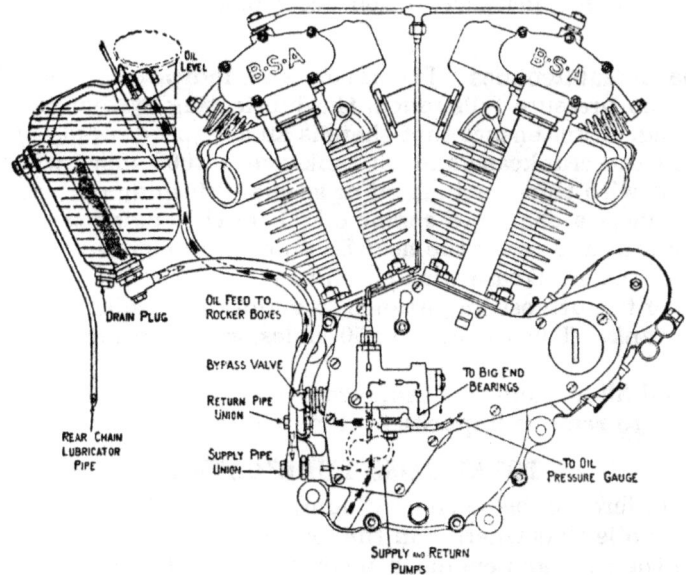

FIG. 13. DRY SUMP LUBRICATION SYSTEM (TYPE D)
Employed on all 1936-8 twin-cylinder engines except those having wet sump lubrication with a mechanical pump

Type D (1936-8 498, 748 c.c. Twin-cylinder Models). The same type of dry sump lubrication system is used on the 1936 Model J12, and the 1936-8 Models Y13. In the case of the 1936-9 986 c.c. S.V. Model G14, however, wet sump lubrication is employed (see page 22).

The oil container is mounted on the right, under the saddle, and a gear-type pump, driven from the timing-side main shaft, draws oil from the tank, and delivers it to the big-end bearings through the mainshaft, flywheel, and crankpin. Direct oil feeds are taken to the rocker gear, push-rods and cams. The other parts are lubricated by splash and the oil, which drains to the bottom of the crankcase, is picked up by the flywheels and collected in a reservoir at the rear of the crankcase by the action of a scraper on the flywheel rims. The oil is then returned by a second set of gears in the pump, to the tank.

The oil flow is indicated by a pressure gauge in the tank. The normal readings are 5-12 lb. per sq. in.

These figures are quite arbitrary, and one should judge rather on the general running of the engine than on the gauge reading as to whether the lubrication is satisfactory. There should be just a puff of bluish smoke from the exhaust when the throttle is opened suddenly after the engine has been running slowly for a while as, for instance, when accelerating after idling behind traffic.

Type D-Maintenance. The gauge is an indicator of the oil flow and if the pressure falls much, the lubricating system should be examined. First ensure that there is an adequate supply of oil.

Drain the crankcase and oil tank every 2000 miles when hot, flush out with thin machine oil or special "flushing oil," and give the cylinders a charge of engine oil. Run the engine slowly for a few minutes and cover the next 50 miles at moderate speeds. Do not flush the crankcase with paraffin.

It is of the utmost importance to maintain an adequate supply in the tank. Top up every 250 miles with suitable engine oil (page 12).

The oil filter should be removed every 2000 miles and washed in petrol to remove impurities. Dry before replacing.

TOTAL LOSS LUBRICATION

The difference between dry sump and total loss wet sump lubrication is that whereas in the former case the whole of the oil in both the tank and engine is in constant circulation, in the latter case the oil in the tank is fed to the engine but is not returned. It is thus commonly called a "total loss" wet sump system. Two total loss oil systems have been used on B.S.A. machines from 1936 onwards and for convenience these will be referred to as types E, F. Both types have a pump adjustment.

Type E (1936-9 986 c.c. Twins). The popular S.V. Big Twin (Model G14) employs a simple but perfectly efficient lubrication system. A duplex Pilgrim mechanical pump is fed with oil from the large oil tank mounted below the saddle. Both pumps are quite independent but are fed by a single supply pipe as may be seen in Fig. 14. A separate adjustment is provided for each pump.

The outer pump, with its control at the front, supplies the big-end bearings and other parts. The inner pump, with its control at the rear, supplies the front cylinder. Each control is adjustable and turning anti-clockwise increases the flow. The oil can be seen flowing in the small chambers visible through the openings at the top of the pump; the chambers are adjacent to their respective controls.

Type E—Maintenance. If it is necessary to remove the pump plungers, damage will result if an attempt is made without first removing the worm. It is important that when reassembling, the plungers are replaced in the same position and direction as removed. Do not revolve the driving worm when end plates are removed from the pump body.

The use of dirty oil will result in rapid wear of the worm and damage to the plunger.

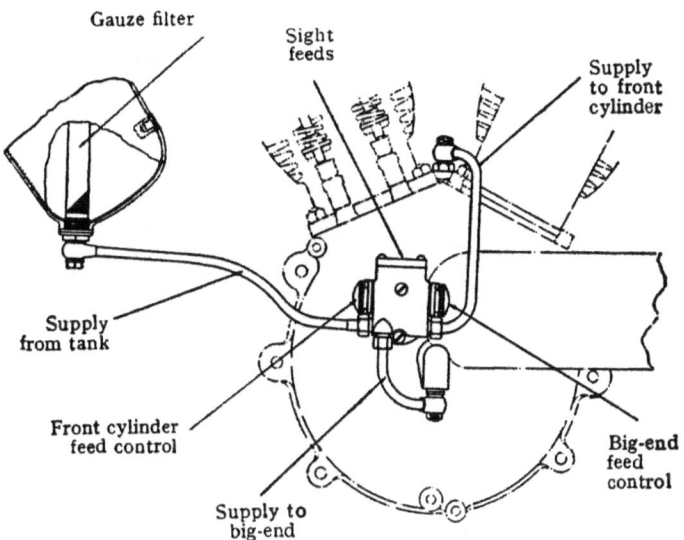

FIG. 14. TOTAL LOSS LUBRICATION SYSTEM (TYPE E)
Used only on 1936-9 twin-cylinder models with mechanical pumps

The rate of flow should be adjusted to suit the general conditions of use. For low speed work the supply can be reduced, and for high speed duty it should be increased, but for general purposes a flow of not more than six drops per minute from each sight-feed when ticking over is necessary. This should give 10-12 drops per minute at normal running speeds. During the running-in period (or first 1000 miles) 25 per cent more oil should be given, and subsequently the quantities should be adjusted to give satisfactory running, as the above figures are arbitrary. The correct setting for any conditions is best determined by experience.

There should be a puff of blue smoke visible at the exhaust when accelerating sharply after running slowly.

Top up the oil tank with suitable engine oil (page 12) about every 250 miles and drain and flush out the crankcase about every 2000 miles, when the oil is warm. With a total loss lubrication system it is not so important to keep the oil tank well filled as in the case of the dry sump system, because the oil in the tank does not circulate and become hot. But there must always be sufficient oil to supply the duplex pump. Use flushing oil, not paraffin, when flushing out the crankcase, and put some fresh oil in before starting up. It will take some time before the oil pump forces sufficient oil into the engine. After flushing, run up the engine gradually and go steady for 50 miles.

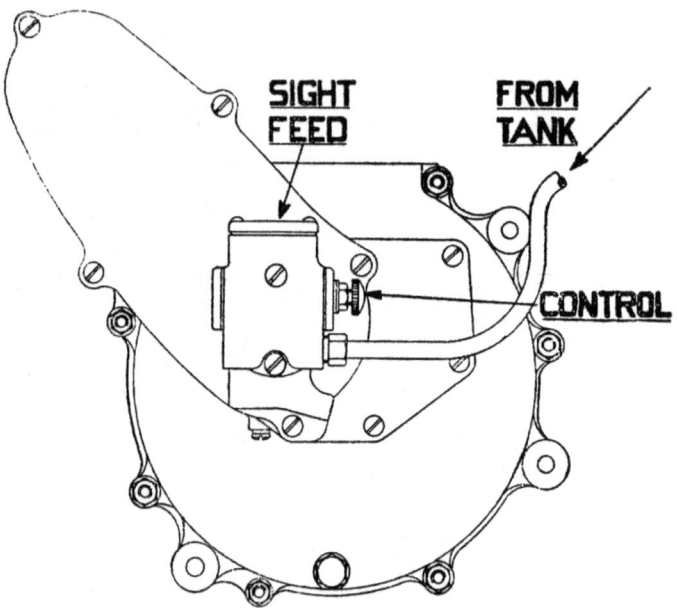

Fig. 15. Total Loss Lubrication System (Type F)
Provided on four 1936 singles (see below)

Type F (1936 149, 249 c.c. Singles). Mechanical pump lubrication is used on the 1936 S.V. Model B1 and the O.H.V. Models B2, B18, X0. The system is extraordinarily simple, the pump being a single plunger Pilgrim type with only one external oil pipe. Oil is gravity-fed from the front compartment of the tank and delivered to the engine by the pump which is mounted on the timing cover. The pump plunger has a combined rotary and reciprocating movement and forces oil up into a sight-feed before delivering it into the engine. A control knob is provided on the right-hand side.

Type F—Maintenance. Top up the oil tank every 250 miles with suitable engine oil (page 12) and keep an eye on the sight-feed where the oil may be observed issuing from the beak in drops.

For normal usage adjust the control to give 14-16 drops of oil per minute. These figures, however, are only intended as a guide and the state of the exhaust, engine behaviour, etc., should be regarded as the best evidence of correct or incorrect lubrication. Drain the crankcase every 1000 miles when the oil is warm, flush out with flushing oil, insert a little engine oil in the cylinder and increase the oil supply above normal until 50 miles have been covered.

To ensure proper working of the Pilgrim pump it is essential to keep the pipe joints, and joint between the pump and engine, oil-tight, and to keep the pump joints air-tight. Use a paper washer between the pump and engine and see that the oil hole is kept clear. If it is necessary to remove the pump plunger, first of all remove the driving worm, bush, and end plate and withdraw the plunger from the left-hand side. If the sight-feed tends to fill up, increase the oil supply temporarily and if this fails to cure matters, clean the ball valve. Chronic filling up is sometimes due to wear of the end cam.

On the O.H.V. Models (B2, B18, X0) the overhead rockers should be lubricated with a grease-gun and the push-rod upper ends with an oil-can about every 250 miles.

THE "MAGDYNO," DYNAMO, ETC.

"Magdyno" Lubrication. Every Lucas "Magdyno" during assembly has the bearings and gear wheels packed with grease, and for this reason no lubricators are provided on the instrument. After many thousands of miles' running, however, the "Magdyno" should be returned to the makers for dismantling, cleaning, and repacking of the bearings with grease.

In order, however, to minimize wear of the fibre heel of the (ring cam type) contact breaker, provision is made for the oiling of the ring cam. A pocket in the contact breaker housing contains a length of felt soaked in oil, and in the ring cam there is a hole fitted with a wick to enable the oil to find its way on to the ring cam surface. It is advisable every 3000 miles to withdraw the ring cam and place a few drops of *thin* oil on the felt. If this is done, it will be found that the magneto will run for long periods without it being necessary to adjust the contacts (Fig. 20).

The Later "Magdyno." The ignition portion now has a face cam type contact breaker (Fig. 37) and the cam is lubricated by a wick in the base of the contact breaker. A few drops of thin machine oil should be added about every 3000 miles. By removing the spring arm carrying the moving contact the wick screw can be withdrawn. At the same time remove the tappet which operates the contact-breaker spring and lightly smear the same with a little thin machine oil. When replacing the arm, see that the small backing spring is fitted correctly with the bent portion facing outwards and immediately after the securing screw and spring washer. On some "Magdynos" a lubricator is provided on the commutator end bracket and a few drops of thin oil should be added every 2000-3000 miles (see Fig. 19).

Dynamo Lubrication (Coil Ignition Models). The armature bearings of the Lucas dynamo fitted on the 1938-9 Models C10, C11, are packed with grease on assembly and this should suffice until your B.S.A. is taken down for a general overhaul, at which time the dynamo should be returned to a Lucas Service Depot for stripping down, cleaning, adjustment, and regreasing. On some Lucas dynamos a lubricator is provided on the commutator end bracket (Fig. 19) and some thin machine oil should be injected every 2000-3000 miles. Use only a few drops. With regard to lubrication of the contact-breaker illustrated in Fig. 38, about every 3000 miles lightly smear the surface of the steel cam with a little Mobilgrease No. 2. Avoid excessive lubrication as oil may get on the contacts and cause pitting and burning. Every 3000 miles the contact-breaker spring and bush (see page 59) should be removed, the rocker lifted off its pivot and the latter smeared with a small quantity of Mobilgrease No. 2.

Automatic Ignition Advance. This is specified on Models C10, C11, and the mechanism requires to be lubricated about every 3000 miles. To do this, remove the cover of the contact-breaker and add a few drops of clean engine oil (see page 12) into the hole in the contact-breaker base through which the cam passes. See that no oil gets on the contacts. To remove the complete mechanism, remove both screws and withdraw it.

Every 3000 miles a few drops of thin machine oil should be inserted through the lubricator provided for the distributor shaft and illustrated in Fig. 38.

Lubrication of Dynamo Chain. This is completely enclosed in the chain case and is automatically lubricated from the timing case. On "Magdyno" models the gears driving the armature are similarly enclosed and automatically lubricated.

Air Cleaners Require Re-oiling. The oil-dip type air cleaners fitted to the carburettors on 1938-9 models should be periodically dismantled, cleaned, and re-oiled. This should be done about every 1000 miles if riding in city areas, every 500 miles in country districts, or about every 250 miles if most of the riding is done on dry, dusty roads. The air cleaner should be dismantled and the filter element washed thoroughly in petrol. Afterwards dry the filter and then submerge it bodily in a light engine oil. Before reassembling, allow the surplus oil to drain off the filter element. 1937 air cleaners require no oiling (see page 6).

THE CYCLE PARTS

Although engine lubrication is the most important, correct lubrication of the cycle parts should never be neglected. A lubrication chart giving the principal points requiring attention is shown in Fig. 16. This chart is wholly applicable to 1937-9 S.V. and O.H.V. singles and mainly applicable to 1936 models. Whatever differences there are, these are explained in this chapter.

Suitable Greases. Grease nipples are provided for those cycle parts which need periodical greasing* and a grease-gun will be found in the tool-kit. Some parts require to be lubricated with engine oil, and in this case oil caps are fitted. It is essential to use only good quality greases. Such greases are: Mobilgrease No. 2, Castrolease Heavy (Medium is also suitable except for the hubs), Shell Retinax CD, Esso Grease, Price's Energrease C1.

Lubrication of Gearbox and Clutch. On all 1936-9 models B.S.A. gearboxes are specified. These are designed to run on *engine oil only.* Suitable brands of oil are given on page 12. The filler plug on the right-hand side of the gearbox should be removed every 500 miles and the oil level checked. If necessary, top up with some engine oil. The correct oil level is such that the gearbox is filled to the level of the filler plug orifice.

In the case of the 1939 250 c.c. S.V. and O.H.V. coil ignition Models C10 De Luxe, C11, however, a separate level plug is provided and after removing *both* plugs oil should be poured in through the filler plug orifice until it begins to flow from the level plug hole. When replenishing a B.S.A. gearbox, first see that the machine is upright and on level ground. Complete filling is assisted by slowly operating the kick-starter several times. After replenishment tighten up the plug(s) securely.

Every 2000 miles place an oil tray beneath the gearbox, remove the drain plug and allow all the oil to drain off. Swill out thoroughly with flushing oil and after replacing the drain plug replenish with fresh oil as described above.

With regard to the clutch, a few drops of oil should be put on the exposed portions of the clutch cable every 500 miles. It is also advisable to lubricate occasionally (about every 1000 miles) the ball in the clutch operation. A grease nipple (*H*, Fig. 50) is provided for this purpose (1936 350, 500 c.c.; all 748, 986 c.c.).

* It is a good plan to go over the greasing points after a long run in wet weather as this forces out water which may have got into the moving parts.

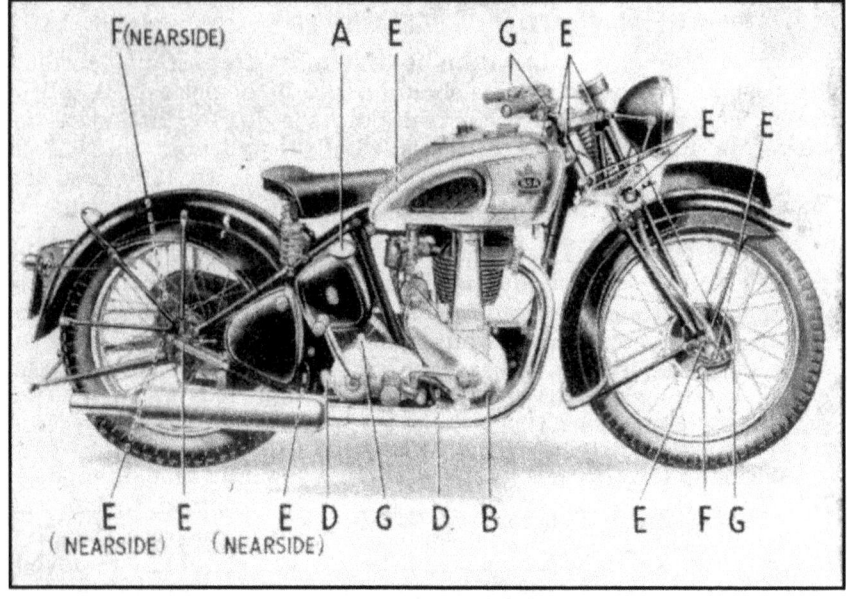

Fig. 16. When and Where to Lubricate

This lubrication chart applies to all 1937-9 single-cylinder dry sump models. Below is a key to letters, also references to page numbers where the various items (1936-9) are dealt with in detail.

A—Oil Tank. Top up if necessary every 250 miles; drain, clean filter every 2000 miles (see pages 16, 17, 22).

B—Engine. Drain, flush out, clean pump filter every 2000 miles (see pages 16, 17, 21, 23).

D—Gearbox. Inspect oil level every 500 miles and top up if necessary; drain and refill every 2000 miles (see page 27).

D—Oil-bath Chain Case. Replenish every 2000 miles (see page 29).

E—Wheel Hubs. Grease every 500 miles with grease gun (see page 31).

E—⎰ *Front Forks.*
⎨ *Steering Head.*
⎨ *Front Saddle Support.* ⎬ Grease every 500 miles with grease-gun (see p. 31).
⎨ *Rear Brake Pedal.*
⎱ *Rear Brake Cam Lever.* ⎭

F—Brake Cams. Grease or oil sparingly every 1000 miles (see page 31).

G—⎰ *Brake Operation.*
⎨ *Exposed Cables.* ⎬ Oil sparingly every 500 miles (see pages 31-32).
⎱ *All Control Rod Joints.* ⎭

Primary Chain Lubrication. All 1937-9 models and the 1936 "Empire Star" models have the primary chain completely enclosed in an oil-bath chain case (Figs. 17, 18). On other 1936 singles (i.e. excluding the "Empire Stars") the primary chain is lubricated by an oil well in the chain case. Oil is fed from an adjustable valve communicating with the crankcase on all 1936 singles over 350 c.c. and the 1936-8 498, 748 c.c. twin-cylinder

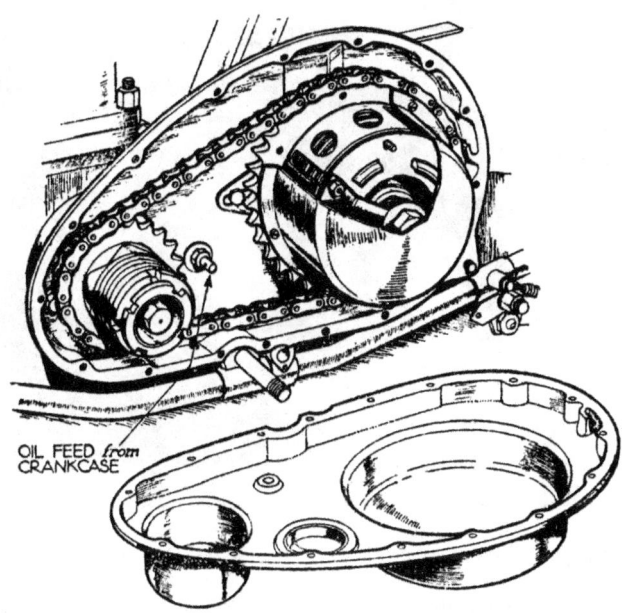

FIG. 17. SHOWING THE ALUMINIUM OIL-BATH CHAIN CASE FITTED TO THE 1936 "EMPIRE STAR" MODELS
Observe the non-adjustable oil feed and the flanged cover which protects the clutch plates from oil
(*From "The Motor Cycle"*)

models. On 1936-9 986 c.c. Twins the feed is from **a breather** valve which is non-adjustable. Other 1936-9 models except Model C10 have no automatic lubrication, but an oil-bath chain-case.

To ensure correct lubrication, about every 2000 miles (every 500 miles on 1936 "Empire Stars") check the level of oil in the oil-bath, draining off any surplus oil or replenishing with some fresh engine oil (see page 12) as required. The level of the oil in the oil-bath is correct when, with the machine upright on level ground, the oil level reaches to (and begins to trickle from) the hexagon plug orifice situated below the foot-rests on the outer half of the chain case. Replenish through the inspection cover, and while doing this keep the level plug removed, otherwise the oil-bath may be over filled and thereby cause a tendency to clutch slip. Slip due to oil getting on the clutch plates (especially where fabric inserts are used) is, however, less likely to occur on the 1936 "Empire Star" machines than on other models because in the former case special protection for the clutch is provided (see Fig. 17). About once every 5000 miles it is a good plan to drain off the whole of the oil and replenish as described above.

Fig. 18. The Pressed-steel Oil-bath Chain Case Used on the 1937-9 Singles (Except Model C10)
Note also the 6 adjuster nuts for the multiple-plate cork insert clutch

Where the chain runs fully protected in an oil-bath, it keeps clean for a long period and removal for cleaning is necessary only after very considerable mileages.

Where an oil-bath chain case is not specified, it is desirable to remove the chain about every 2000 miles and clean and grease it thoroughly as described in the next paragraph.

Secondary Chain Lubrication. Where an oil-bath primary chain case is fitted, on some models the secondary chain is automatically lubricated by an adjustable feed at the rear of the primary chain case. Where no automatic lubrication is provided it is desirable to smear grease with a brush on to the chain about every 1000 miles. On no account allow the chain to run dry.

Engine oil can be used for the rear chain, and the best method of oiling is to rotate the chain with the wheel and apply an oil-gun or can to the top of the chain. See that the oil is falling upon the rollers, and not on the ground, and make a practice of oiling regularly. If the chain be neglected, undue wear of both chain and sprockets will ensue, and the transmission will be harsh. From time to time (say once every 2000 miles) take off the chain and give it a bath in paraffin. If allowed to soak well, the whole of the dirt will be extracted, and the chain may be hung up to dry and refitted. Before refitting, however, the wisest course is to immerse the chain in a receptacle containing a mixture of warm graphite and Mobilgrease No. 2, which will then permeate all the roller bearings. There is no better treatment for a main driving chain, although plain engine oil or regular greasing will answer satisfactorily. After it has cooled, wipe off the excess lubricant. Under load the lubricant will be gradually squeezed out; the process should therefore be repeated about every 3000 miles. Clean the sprockets and, on replacing the chain, note that the split end of the spring fastener faces opposite to the direction of travel of the chain.

The Transmission Shock-absorber. No lubrication of the engine shaft shock-absorber (Fig. 17) is needed, as this, being enclosed in the chain case, is adequately lubricated by oil thrown off the primary chain.

Grease the Wheel Hubs. Ball bearing hubs are provided on many 250 c.c. models, but on all 250 c.c. de Luxe models, most 350 c.c. models and all machines of 500 c.c. and over the wheels have taper roller bearing hubs. The bearings (including the rear sprocket bearing on the 1936 498 c.c. model), whether they be of the ball or roller type, require to be greased about every 1000 miles. Apply the grease-gun to the nipples provided and give several strokes for each wheel. Where a sidecar is fitted, do not forget to grease the wheel of the sidecar. It is most important to keep the hubs well greased because the bearings are called upon to do heavy duty, but do not inject excessive grease, otherwise some of it may find its way on to the brake linings and reduce braking efficiency. Fine weather riders need lubricate less often.

—Also the Fork Spindles and Steering Head. To ensure sweet fork action, the fork spindles and the ball bearings in the steering head should be greased about every 500 miles. Grease nipples are provided. Neglect of the steering head bearings is apt to cause an objectionable stiffness and possibly damage to the ball races.

Front Saddle Support. On some machines, including 1937-9 500, 600 c.c. models, a grease nipple is provided for the front support of the saddle and several strokes of the gun should be given every 500 miles.

Lubrication of Brakes. About every 1000 miles grease the brake cams of both wheels, where grease nipples are provided. On some machines the cams are intended to be oiled. This applies to the 1939 Models C10, C11. Exposed brake cable ends, brake rod joints, levers, etc., should be lubricated with a few drops of oil every 500 miles. Grease the rear brake pedal and cam lever

—Do Not Forget Also. Every 500 miles also put a few drops of oil on the exposed parts of the carburettor cables, levers, the exhaust valve lifter cable, the gear control, etc. When fitting new cables, charge the casings with thin grease or oil, which may be done with a piece of rubber tubing and a grease-gun.

The Speedometer Drive. About every 5000 miles disconnect the flexible drive from the speedometer gearbox beside the front wheel and grease it thoroughly with one of the greases mentioned on page 27.

Lubrication of Dipper Switch. Every 5000 miles lubricate the moving parts of the dipper switch with a little thin machine oil.

Lubrication Points on Sidecar. Do not forget the sidecar hub where a sidecar is fitted. Also every 250 miles apply the grease-gun to the rear spring and shackle link bolts.

Gearbox Lubricants (1936 Onwards). Replenish the gearbox with *engine oil* (see page 12). Use the correct grades recommended for summer and winter use.

CHAPTER III

CARE OF LIGHTING SYSTEM

LUCAS electric lighting equipment has been specified on all 1936 B.S.A. models onwards and comprises, except on 1938 and later 250 c.c. Models C10, C11, 1936 Model XO, a "Magdyno," headlamp, tail lamp, instrument panel (on some models), and a lead-acid battery. Models C10, C11 have coil ignition, a dynamo replacing the "Magdyno." This, however, is of identical design to the dynamo portion of the "Magdyno." Model XO has a "Maglita."

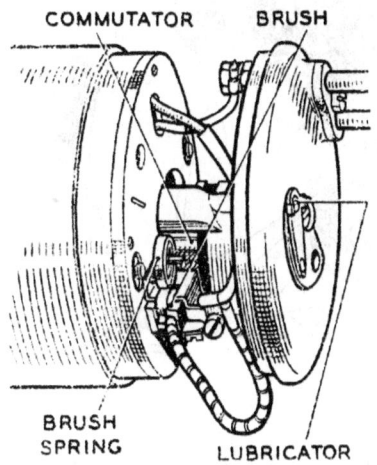

FIG. 19. COMMUTATOR END OF THE LUCAS DYNAMO OR DYNAMO PORTION OF THE "MAGDYNO" (1937 ONWARDS)
Some thin machine oil should be put in the lubricator (where fitted) about every 2000-3000 miles

The Lucas "Magdyno." This consists of a magneto and a 6-volt dynamo strapped together to form a single unit. The dynamo can if necessary be detached and the magneto half used only. In this case a protective cover (obtainable from the makers) must be fitted over the gears to exclude dirt. All 1936 and earlier "Magdynos" and dynamos operate on the "third brush" method of output control. but on 1937, later types, compensated voltage control is fitted. With this arrangement the cut-out is mounted separately from the dynamo, only two brushes are fitted, and charging is entirely automatic (see page 40). A conversion set may be obtained for pre-1937 dynamos.

DYNAMO MAINTENANCE

Before removing the cover (except C.V.C.), it is necessary to disconnect the positive lead of the battery to avoid the danger of reversing the polarity of the dynamo or short-circuiting the

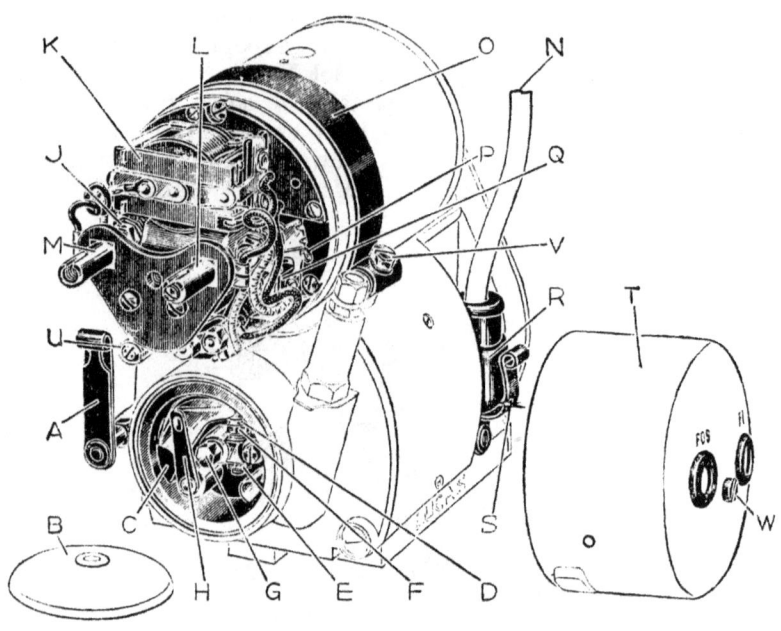

Fig. 20. 1935-6 Lucas "Magdyno" with Cut-out (see Fig. 19)

A = Securing spring for contact-breaker cover
B = Contact-breaker cover
C = Fibre heel
D = Contact points
E = Locking nut
F = Adjustable contact point
G = Contact-breaker fixing screw
H = Locating spring
J = Nut securing brush eyelet
K = Cut-out
L = Terminal marked "F1"
M = Terminal marked "POS"
N = Cable to sparking plug
O = Dynamo securing strap
P = Spring lever holding brush in position
Q = Carbon brush
R = H.T. pick-up
S = Securing spring for pick-up
T = Commutator cover
U = Earthing terminal
V = Screw securing dynamo strap
W = Commutator cover fixing screw

battery, either of which might cause serious damage. To disconnect, push back the rubber shield and unscrew the cable connector, being careful not to touch the frame with the cable and cause a short circuit. When reconnecting, make sure the rubber shield is pulled well over the connector.

CARE OF LIGHTING SYSTEM   35

If at any time the motor-cycle must be ridden with the battery disconnected, or in any way out of service, it is essential to run with the switch in the "OFF" position (compensated voltage control excepted).

Brushes. Every 5000-6000 miles remove the dynamo cover or the band and inspect the brushgear and commutator. It is very important to make sure that the brushes work freely in their holders. This can be easily ascertained by holding back the spring lever and gently pulling each flexible lead, when the brush should move without the slightest suggestion of sluggishness. It should also return to its original position directly the lead is let go. When testing the brush in this way, release it gently, otherwise it may get chipped. The brushes should be clean and "bed" over the whole surface; that is, the face in contact with the commutator should appear uniformly polished. Dirty or sticking brushes may be cleaned with a cloth moistened with petrol.

If the brushes become so badly worn that it is necessary to remove them, this can easily be done as follows: Release the eyelet on the brush lead by unscrewing the hexagonal nut or screw at the terminal; then, holding back the spring lever out of the way, withdraw the brush from its holder. Renew with genuine Lucas brushes.

The brush springs should be inspected occasionally to see that they have sufficient tension to keep the brushes firmly pressed against the commutator when the machine is running. It is particularly necessary to keep this in mind when the brushes have been in use a long time and are very much worn down. Owners are cautioned that it is unwise to insert brushes of a grade other than that supplied with the machine, or to change the tension springs. The arrangement provided has been made only after many years' experience, and will be found to give the best results and the longest life. It is really best when the brushes become so worn that they no longer bed down on the commutator, to go to a Lucas Service Depot, as this ensures the brushes being properly "bedded."

Commutator Must be Clean. The surface of the commutator should be kept clean and free from oil or brush dust, etc. Should any grease or oil work its way on to the commutator through over-lubrication, it will not only cause sparking, but, in addition, carbon and copper dust will be collected in the grooves between the commutator segments. The best way to clean the commutator is, without disconnecting any leads, to remove from its box one of the main brushes and, inserting a dry duster in the box, hold it, by means of a suitably-shaped piece of wood, against the commutator surface, causing the armature to be rotated at the same time. If very dirty, moisten the duster with petrol. If the commutator has been neglected for long periods, it may need cleaning with fine glasspaper, but this is more difficult to do, and should not be necessary if it has received regular attention.

Dynamo Terminals. The positive dynamo terminal, marked "POS," and the shunt-field terminal, marked "FI," are situated on either side of the cover (Fig. 20). To connect up, the cables merely have to be bared and clamped in their terminals by means of grub-screws.

On the later "Magdyno" (Fig. 19) with separate voltage control unit the positive dynamo terminal is marked "D" and the shunt-field terminal "F" on the cover. To connect up, first slacken the fixing screw on the terminal block and remove the clamping plate. Then withdraw the metal sleeve from each terminal. The cables should then be passed through the clamping plate holes and bared at the ends for $\frac{3}{8}$ in. Now fit the sleeves over the cables, bend back the wires over them and push the sleeves home into the terminals, finally screwing down the clamping plate.

Electro-magnetic Cut-out. The cut-out automatically closes by means of solenoids the charging circuit, as soon as the dynamo voltage rises above that of the battery. When the dynamo voltage falls below that of the battery, the reverse action takes place, that is, the cut-out opens and thereby prevents the battery from discharging itself through the dynamo. Leave cut-out alone. The cut-out is accurately set before leaving the works.

Absence of Fuses. In order to simplify the system as far as possible, no fuse is provided. If all the connexions are kept clean and tight, there is no possibility of any excess current causing damage to the equipment.

Ammeter. This gives a reading of the amount of current flowing into or from the battery and shows whether the equipment is functioning satisfactorily. It is of the centre-zero type.

CARE OF THE BATTERY (LEAD-ACID TYPE)

It is of the utmost importance that the battery should receive regular attention to keep it in good condition.

The following are the most important maintenance hints—

1. Keep the acid level with the tops of the separators.

CARE OF LIGHTING SYSTEM

2. Add only distilled water, never tap water.
3. Test the condition of the battery by taking readings of the specific gravity of the acid with a hydrometer.
4. Never leave the battery in a discharged condition.

Topping-up. At least once a month the filler caps on top of the battery should be removed and the level of the acid solution* examined. If necessary, distilled water, which can be obtained at all chemists and most garages, should be added to bring the acid level with the tops of the separators. Top up with a small syringe or a battery filler. If, however, acid solution has been spilled, it should be replaced by diluted sulphuric acid solution of the same specific gravity. It is important when examining the cells that naked lights should not be held near the vents, on account of the possible danger of igniting the gas coming from the plates. At monthly intervals or if acid has been spilled, test the specific gravity with a hydrometer. The S.G. should be 1·280-1·300, fully charged; about 1·210, about half discharged; below 1·150, fully discharged. These figures assume a temperature of 60° F. All the cells should give the same reading unless acid has been spilled or there is a short.

Storage. If the equipment is laid by for several months, the battery must be given a small charge from a separate source of electrical energy about once a fortnight, in order to obviate any permanent sulphation of the plates. In no circumstances must the electrolyte be removed from the battery and the plates allowed to dry, as certain chemical changes take place which result in permanent loss of capacity.

Battery-charging Period. Overcharging is less injurious than undercharging. It is difficult to lay down rigid instructions on this subject, as the conditions under which motor-cycles are used vary considerably; and, obviously, the amount of charging a battery will require is directly dependent on the current used. The following suggestions will serve as a rough guide where compensated voltage control is not fitted.

The switch should be left in the C position for about 1 hour daily. This time should only be increased if the period of night running is considerable, or when the battery is found to be in a low state of charge (if the specific gravity of the acid solution is 1·210 or below). Where a sidecar is fitted and/or an electric horn, considerably more charging may be necessary. Overcharging will cause nothing worse than loss of acid by gassing, but undercharging may spoil the battery by causing sulphation of the plates.

* The electrolyte consists of water and acid, but only the water evaporates.

38   BOOK OF THE B.S.A.

The battery must never be left in a fully-discharged condition, and unless some long runs are to be taken, it is advisable to have the battery removed from the machine and charged up from an independent electrical supply.

LAMPS

The DU Type Headlamp. This lamp, used on most 1936-39 B.S.A.'s with no instrument panel, is fitted with a double filament

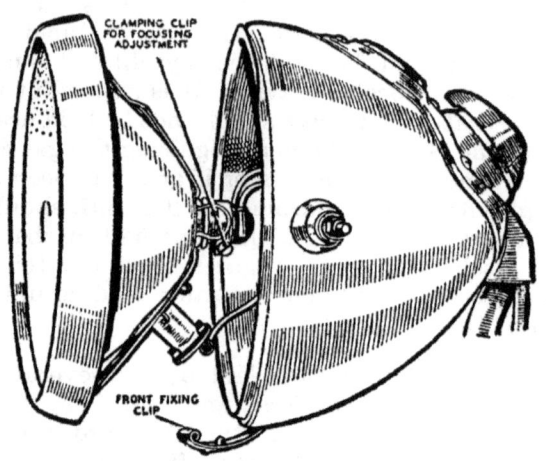

FIG. 21. LUCAS DU TYPE HEADLAMP

bulb, the one filament providing the normal driving light, while the second one gives an anti-dazzle dipped beam. The change-over from the normal driving light to the dipped beam is made by a handlebar switch. A small pilot bulb is provided for use when the machine is stationary or when driving in town.

An ammeter is incorporated in the lamp, which gives the driver an indication of the amount of current in amperes by which the battery is being charged or discharged under the various conditions governed by the particular position of the switch. When the lamp is switched on, the ammeter is indirectly illuminated.

The D Type Headlamp. This headlamp is used on the 1936-39 B.S.A. models with an instrument panel and is very similar to the DU headlamp, but it contains neither switch nor ammeter, these being housed on the instrument panel. As with the DU headlamp, a double filament bulb is used, one filament (for normal driving light) being placed at the focus of the reflector, and the other (for dipped beam) being situated slightly above it. A small pilot bulb is also incorporated for parking purposes and when driving in well-illuminated streets. The panel switch positions are the same as for the DU lamp.

Switch Positions. The lighting switch screwed to the back of the lamp or instrument panel has the following positions—
"Off"—Lamps off, and dynamo not charging.
C—Lamps off and dynamo giving half its normal output.
H—Headlamp (driving light), tail lamp, speedometer, and sidecar lamp on; dynamo giving maximum output (4-5 amp.).
L—With the exception that the pilot light is in the place of

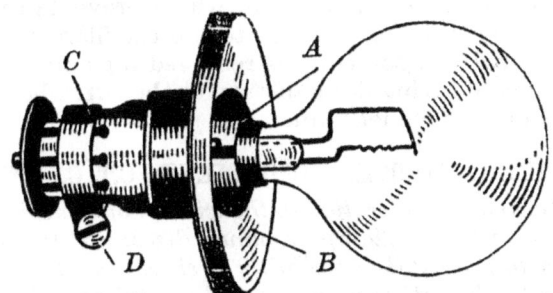

FIG. 22. SHOWING DETAILS OF LUCAS BULB-HOLDER
The headlamps on 1936-39 models have this type of holder fitted. At *A, B, C, D* are shown respectively the bulb-holder, the holder support, the clamping clip, and the clamping screw

the driving light, the conditions are exactly the same as in position *H*. On 1937 and later models provided with compensated voltage control the "*C*" position is omitted (page 46).

How to Clean Lucas Lamps. Reflectors should be cleaned by polishing lightly with a chamois leather or a soft cloth. Never use metal polish. With regard to the lamp exterior, clean ebony black lamps with a good car polish. To remove dirt from chromium surfaces wash with plenty of water. Then polish with a chamois leather or a soft dry cloth.

Focusing DU and D Type Headlamps. The best way of focusing and setting the lamp is to take the motor-cycle to a straight, level road; find the correct bulb adjustment and then move the lamp on its adjustable mounting until the main beam is parallel to the road. On machines with or without an instrument panel the focusing of the headlamp is carried out in the same manner. To focus the main bulb it is necessary to remove the lamp front and reflector by pressing back the fixing clip. Then slacken the clamping screw which secures the bulb-holder and move the bulb-holder and bulb (Fig. 22) until correct focus is obtained (on a wall 30-40 ft away). Afterwards tighten the clamping screw. To remove the bulb-holder, press back the two securing springs. When replacing the lamp front and reflector the top of the rim should be located first. See that the earthing clip makes good contact with the back of the reflector. For bulbs, see page 47.

Sidecar Lamp. By unscrewing the locating screw at the bottom of the rim, the lamp front and reflector may be removed. The top of the rim should be located first when replacing.

Tail Lamp (All Except some of Smaller Models). The bulb-holder is mounted on a rubber diaphragm, which prevents road and engine vibration from being transmitted to the filament.

The rear portion of the lamp is removed for bulb replacements by pushing in and giving it a half-turn to the left, when it becomes detached from its bayonet fixing.

WIRING OF THE EQUIPMENT, C.V.C., ETC.

Before making any alteration to the wiring, or removing the switch from the back of the headlamp or panel, disconnect the positive lead at the battery to prevent the possibility of short circuits. See page 34.

All cables to the DU type headlamp are taken directly into the switch, which can be easily withdrawn from the lamp body when the three fixing screws are removed.

The ends of 1936-39 cables are identified by means of coloured sleevings as shown on the wiring diagrams. When making a connexion, proceed as follows: bare about ¾ in. of the cable, twist the wire strands together, and turn back about ⅛ in. so as to form a small ball. Remove the grub screw from the appropriate terminal and insert the wire so that the ball fits in the terminal post. Now replace and tighten the grub-screw; this will compress the ball to make a good electrical connexion.

Compensated Voltage Control. This is used on all 1937 and later B.S.A.'s. Wiring diagrams are given on pages 41-5.

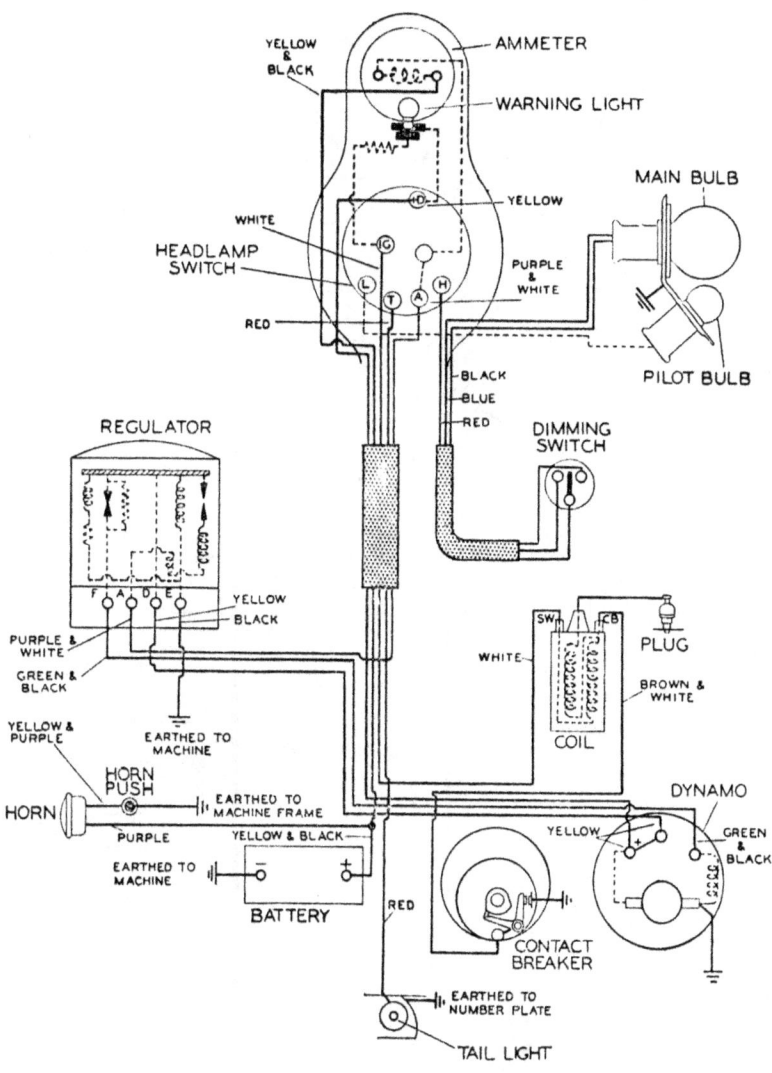

(*Messrs. Joseph Lucas, Ltd.*)

Fig. 23. Wiring Diagram for Lucas 1939 Dynamo Lighting and Coil Ignition Equipment with Automatic Voltage Control
All internal connexions are shown dotted and the W.D. applies only to 1938-9 coil ignition Models C10, C11

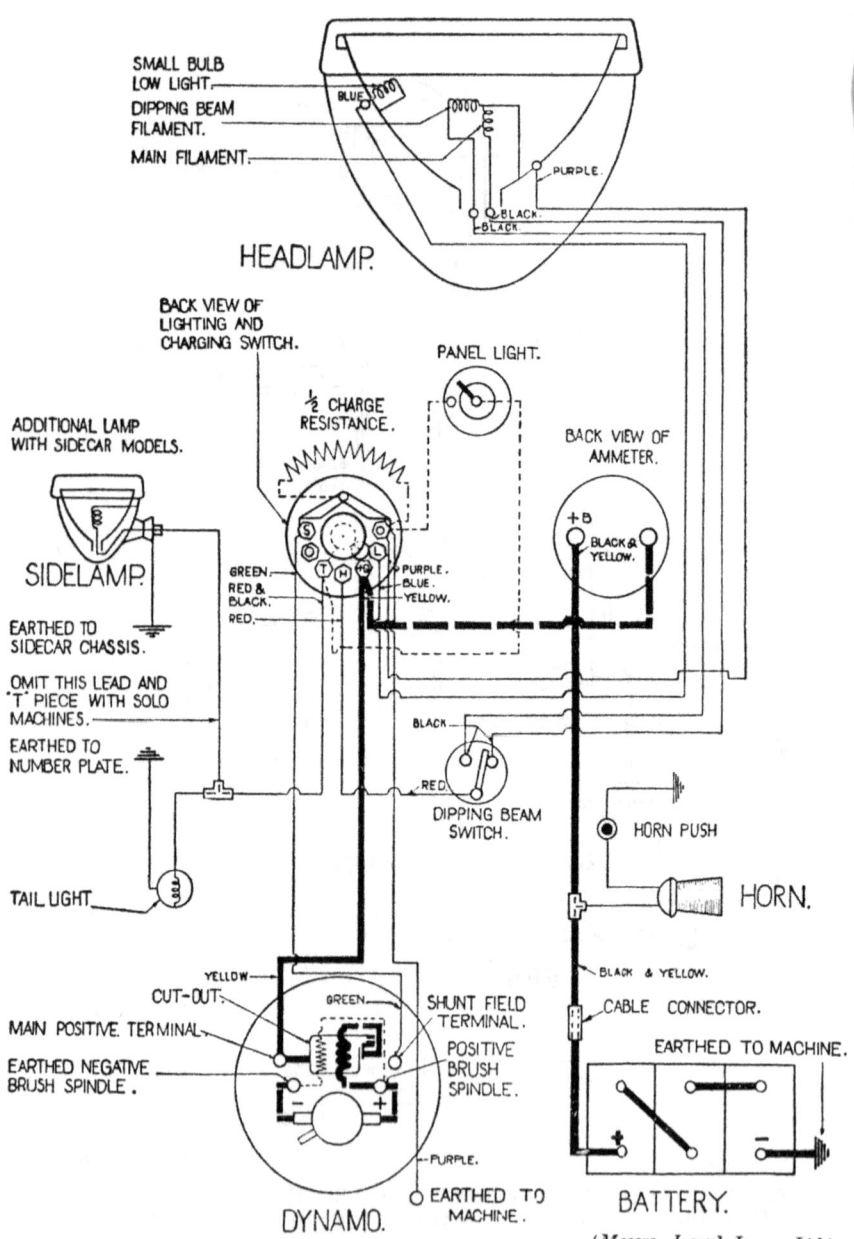

FIG. 24. WIRING DIAGRAM FOR THE 1936 LUCAS "MAGDYNO" LIGHTING EQUIPMENT WITH INSTRUMENT PANEL, WITHOUT AUTOMATIC VOLTAGE CONTROL

A W.D. for the "Magdyno" equipment without instrument panel will be found opposite

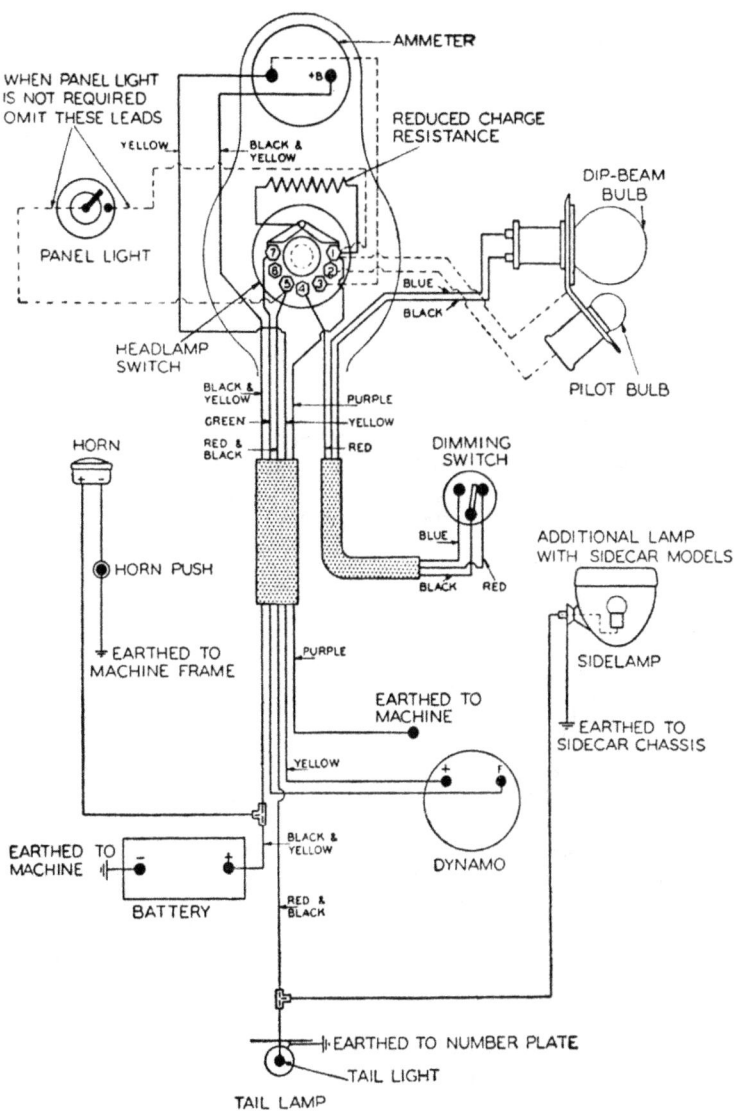

Fig. 25. Wiring Diagram for 1936 Lucas "Magdyno" Lighting Equipment Without Instrument Panel, Without Automatic Voltage Control

All internal connexions are shown dotted

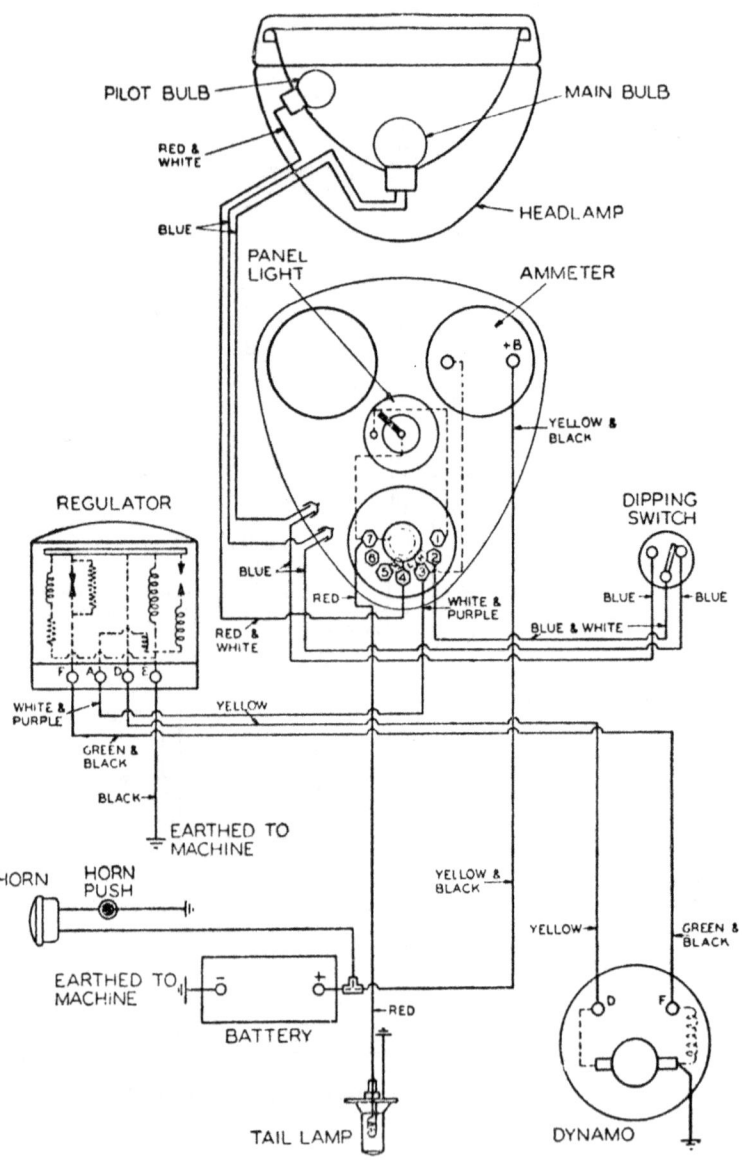

Fig. 26. Wiring Diagram for 1937-9 "Magdyno" Lighting Equipment with Instrument Panel with Automatic Voltage Control

All internal connexions are shown dotted. A W.D. for equipment without instrument panel is given opposite

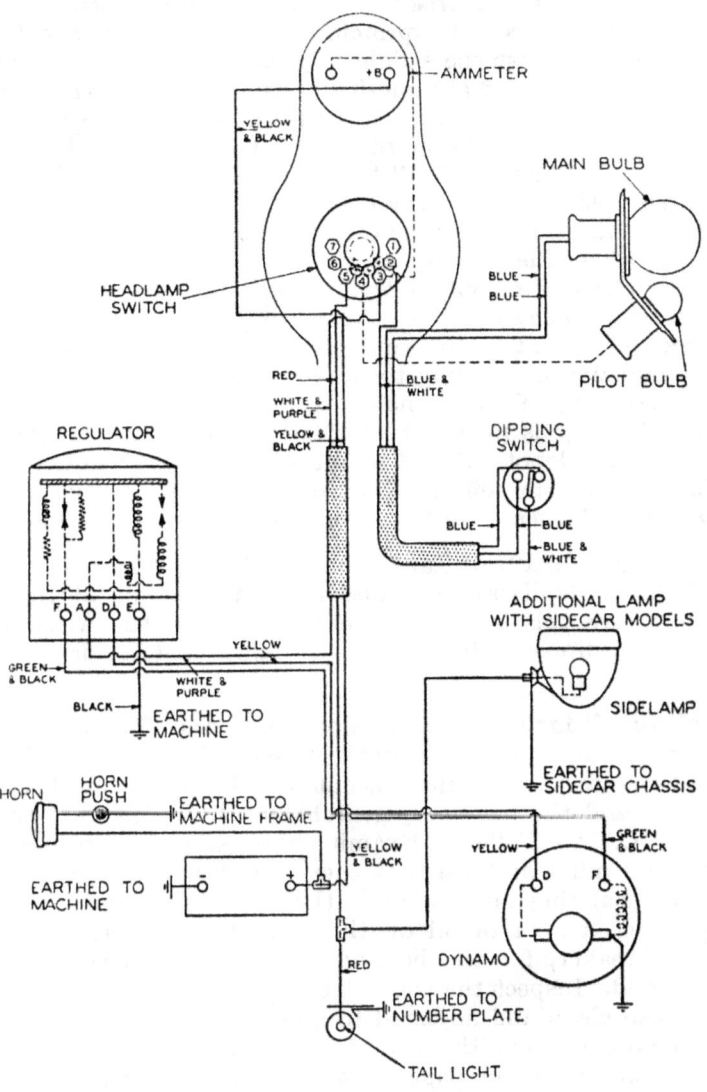

(*Messrs. Joseph Lucas, Ltd.*)

FIG. 27. WIRING DIAGRAM FOR 1937-9 "MAGDYNO" LIGHTING EQUIPMENT WITHOUT INSTRUMENT PANEL, WITH AUTOMATIC VOLTAGE CONTROL

All internal connexions are shown dotted

The control unit comprises the cut-out and voltage control (working on the trembler principle) neatly housed in a box on the mudguard under the saddle. It sees to it that the battery is kept properly charged automatically, the dynamo output varying according to the state of charge of the battery and the load. With this equipment the switch resistance is omitted and there are only three positions—"Off," "L," and "H" for the switch. In all three positions the dynamo gives a controlled output, thus relieving the rider of much responsibility. During daylight running when the battery is well charged the ammeter may indicate a charge of only 1 or 2 amperes, for the dynamo gives only a trickle charge. The voltage control unit is sealed by the makers and should not be tampered with, the only likely trouble being oxidizing or welding together of the contacts due to accidental crossing of the dynamo field and positive leads. If a "Nife" battery is fitted, the regulator should be changed at a Lucas service depot. Excellent service is given at Lucas depots.

Note that on the coil ignition Model C11 a small ignition key is provided in the centre of the lighting switch.

Removing the Petrol Tank. On a B.S.A. with an instrument panel it is not advisable to disconnect the wiring at the panel itself. Leave this end intact and disconnect the wires at the head lamp, dipper switch, horn, tail lamp, and regulator (where fitted).

"Maglita" Lighting and Ignition. A Lucas "Maglita" is fitted on one machine only, the 1936 149 c.c. Model XO. With this equipment an automatic cut-out of the mechanical type is provided and the headlamp switch has the following positions: "Off," "C," "H," "L," Examine the generator brushes every 2000-3000 miles and see that they are clean and free from oil. Also see that they slide freely in their guides. About every 1000 miles place a spot of oil on the cam, in the holes under the contact-breaker, for the bearing, and in the lubricator at the spindle end. Inspect the contact-breaker points occasionally and keep them clean and adjusted to give a "break" of 0·010 in. On no account remove the armature. The battery maintenance instructions given on page 36 are applicable, but it should be noted as regards lamps that the headlamp requires a 12 watt double-filament bulb and other lamps a 3 watt bulb.

BULB RENEWAL

When fitting a new bulb to a Lucas headlamp, always see that the renewal bulb is of Lucas manufacture. Lucas bulbs are specially designed for use in conjunction with Lucas reflectors and another make of bulb will *not* give the best results.

CARE OF LIGHTING SYSTEM

Where a double-filament main (focusing-type) bulb is concerned, it is important to make sure that the bulb is fitted with the dipped-beam filament *above* the centre filament. After fitting a new main bulb it is generally desirable to check the focus of the headlamp (see page 39).

Bulbs for 1936-39 Lamps. For the 1936-39 Lucas DU and D type headlamps, and the Lucas tail lamps, the following are the correct bulb renewals—

Main bulb—6 volt, 24 watt, double-filament, Lucas No. 70.

Pilot (also instrument panel and tail) bulb—6 volt, 3 watt, Lucas No. 200.

CHAPTER IV

OVERHAULING (See Publishers Note - Page 96)

IN this chapter the author has included all essential information about the maintenance and overhauling of 1936-9 models. Reference to carburation, lubrication, and the lighting system has, however, been omitted since these subjects have already been fully discussed. In order to enable the reader to find what he wants quickly, the chapter has been divided into a number of sections.

Cleaning the Machine. The life of the machine is increased and its appearance and value greatly improved by regular and careful attention to cleaning. Special care should be taken near all moving parts, so as to prevent grit working in and causing undue wear and other troubles.

It should be noted that chromium plating does not require and should not be treated with metal polish, for it does not oxidize in the same manner as nickel-plating. The chromium-plated parts should be treated similarly to the enamel, and the surfaces will then improve with cleaning. Polish with a *soft* cloth.

Periodical Inspection of Nuts. One of the most important points in connexion with the care of a motor-cycle is to look over the machine frequently and apply a spanner to any nuts which may have worked loose. It is particularly important to check the tightness of the cylinder head bolts or nuts after decarbonizing and when a machine is new.

VALVE CLEARANCES

It is very important to maintain the correct valve clearances on all B.S.A. engines, and the clearances should be checked about every 700 miles, or more often in the case of new engines where considerable bedding down of the parts occurs, and after grinding-in the valves. It should be noted that incorrect valve clearances interfere with both the lift of the valves and also the valve timing. Excessive clearances result in undue noise and loss of efficiency due to reduced valve lift and late opening of the valves, but no damage to the valves is likely to be caused. Insufficient valve clearances, besides resulting in loss of compression, flexibility, and power, may cause distortion and perhaps burning of the exhaust valve due to gas leakage past it during the power

OVERHAULING

strokes. Experienced riders can usually tell by the sound and "feel" of an engine whether the valve clearances are correct.

Before Checking the Valve Clearances. On all 1936-9 engines it is essential to verify that (a) both valves are fully closed, and (b) there is sufficient clearance at the exhaust valve lifter. To ensure both valves being fully closed and the flat base tappets

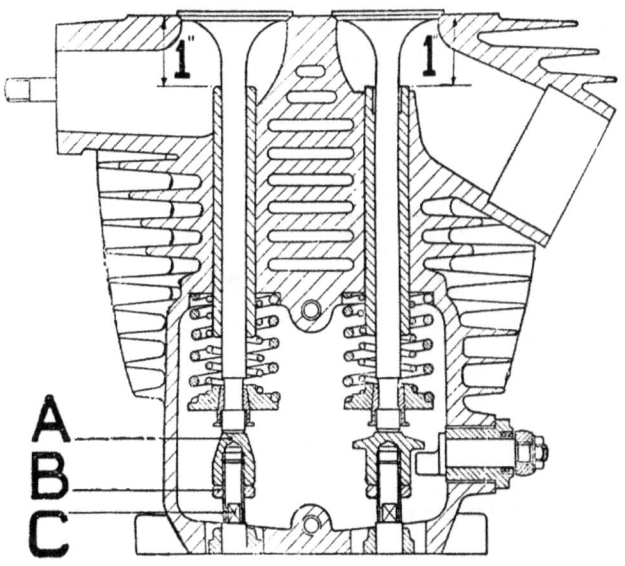

FIG. 28. TAPPET ADJUSTMENT ON 1939 500, 600 C.C. S.V. ENGINES

or cam followers being in contact with the base circle of the cams, first of all (except on the 1939 S.V., O.H.V. Models B21-B26, M20-M24 (see below)) turn the engine over gradually until the inlet valve has just closed and the piston reaches the top of the compression stroke. The best method of obtaining the true T.D.C. position is to remove the sparking plug or the compression plug (fitted on some S.V. engines) and with a pencil or piece of stiff wire feel the position of the piston while gently turning the engine backwards and forwards. In order to turn the engine backwards it is, of course, necessary to engage a gear and move the rear wheel by hand. Having obtained the T.D.C. position, check that the adjustment of the exhaust valve lifter is correct (see page 54) and that the exhaust tappet or rocker is not influenced to the slightest degree by the valve lifter.

(1) Tappet Adjustment (1939 S.V., O.H.V. Models B21-B26, M20-M24). The tappet clearances should always be checked and if necessary adjusted *with the engine cold*. On these machines it is imperative owing to the special cam design to adjust the tappets in a rather unorthodox manner, not by first placing the piston at T.D.C. with both valves closed. The correct procedure is as follows. Remove the tappet inspection cover, taking care not to damage the oil sealing washer. Then rotate the engine slowly, operating the kick-starter by hand until a feeler gauge can be inserted in the clearance space of one of the tappets. Now turn over the B.S.A. engine very slowly, pausing at intervals to insert the gauge until the position is found where there is *maxi-*

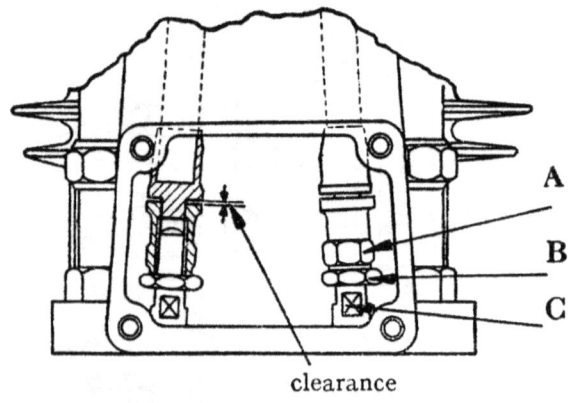

Fig. 29. Tappet Adjustment on 1939 500, 600 c.c. O.H.V. Engines

mum tappet clearance. In this position the tappet clearance should remain constant for an appreciable amount of crankshaft rotation and the clearance should be carefully checked with a feeler gauge of the correct thickness (supplied in the tool-kit), and adjusted if necessary as described in the next paragraph. Deal similarly with the inlet and exhaust tappets. Should it be necessary to turn the engine backwards, engage a gear and move the rear wheel.

Deal separately with each tappet thus: with one spanner hold the tappet head *A* (Figs. 28, 29) and with another loosen the lock-nut *B*. Then with a spanner applied to the flats at *C*, hold the stem of the tappet and screw the tappet head *A* up or down as required in order to obtain the correct clearance. Finally re-tighten the lock-nut *B* securely against the tappet head.

When adjusting the tappets on the O.H.V. engines, except the Standard models, raise the push-rod with the fingers, otherwise its own weight will prevent the feeler gauge from being inserted into the clearance space correctly.

In the case of the 1939 S.V. Model B23 Standard the correct

OVERHAULING

inlet and exhaust clearances are 0·004 in. and 0·008 in. respectively. On the Model B23 de Luxe the correct clearances are 0·008 in. and 0·012 in. respectively. On the 1939 S.V. Models M20, M21, give clearances of 0·010 in. and 0·012 in. respectively.

With regard to the 1939 O.H.V. models, the correct inlet and exhaust valve clearances are 0·003 in. and 0·003 in. for Model B21 Standard, Model M22; 0·003 in. and 0·003 in. for Model M24; 0·006 in. and 0·006 in. for Models M23, B21 de Luxe, B24, B25, B26.

(2) **Tappet Adjustment (1936 S.V. Models B1, M10, W6, 1937-8 S.V. Models M20, M21, 1938-9 S.V. Model C10).** All valve clearances must be checked and if necessary adjusted *with the engine cold.* On the above-mentioned machines it is necessary first to turn over the engine until the piston is at the top of the compression stroke, with both valves closed. Find the true T.D.C. position as described on page 49. Remove the tappet inspection cover and check the inlet and exhaust valve tappet clearances with a feeler gauge of the correct thickness.

If the clearance at either tappet is found to be incorrect, hold the tappet head *A* (Fig. 30) by means of the large end of the B.S.A. spanner provided in the tool-kit, and loosen the lock-nut *B* with another spanner, turning the spanner to the left (clockwise). Then screw the tappet head up or down to the required position, meanwhile holding the stem of the tappet rigid by means of a spanner applied to the flats *C*. Finally re-tighten the lock-nut *B* against the tappet head *A*. After tightening, test the clearance again to make sure that it has not been altered accidentally during the tightening up of the lock-nut. It is well worth while taking some pains to get tappet adjustment perfect, since this makes for mechanical silence and high performance.

Fig. 30. Typical S.V. Tappet Adjustment

With regard to tappet clearances, in the case of the 1936 S.V. Models M10, W6 the inlet and exhaust valve clearances should be 0·004 in. and 0·008 in. respectively. The correct inlet and exhaust valve clearances for the 1936 Model B1, the 1937 Models M20, M21, and the 1938-9 Model C10 are 0·004 in. and 0·006 in. respectively, but on the 1938 Models M20, M21 the exhaust tappet clearance should be not less than 0·012 in.

(3) **Tappet Adjustment (1937-8 S.V., O.H.V. Models B20-B26).** Check and adjust the clearances with the engine *cold*. The

tappet adjustment which is shown in Fig. 31 is effected as follows.

Set the piston at T.D.C. as described on page 49. Remove the tappet cover and then with a spanner applied to the flats at *C* hold the tappet foot while turning lock-nut *B* with a spanner to the right (anti-clockwise). Now turn the tappet head *A*, holding *C* firm, until the correct tappet clearance is obtained. Finally tighten lock-nut *B* against *C*, not *A* as in the case of the models dealt with in section (2).

The correct inlet and exhaust valve clearances for the S.V.

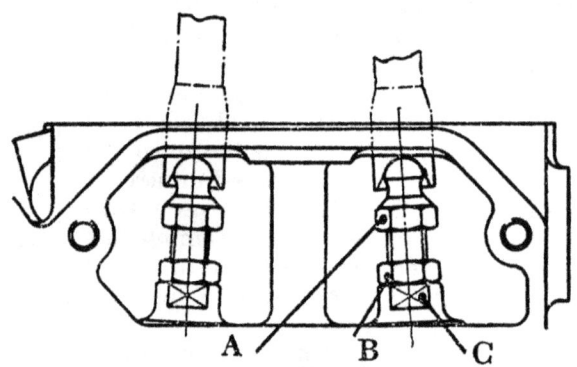

FIG. 31. TAPPET ADJUSTMENT ON 1937-8 250, 350 C.C. O.H.V. ENGINES

Models B20, B23 are 0·004 in. and 0·006 in. respectively, but on the 1938 Model B23 give an exhaust tappet clearance of not less than 0·008 in.

On all 1937-8 O.H.V. models of the "B" class the correct tappet adjustment is such that the tappet can be rotated freely between the thumb and finger, with just perceptible up and down movement. This applies to both inlet and exhaust tappets.

(4) **Tappet Adjustment (All 1936-9 S.V. Twins).** With the engine *cold*, check and adjust the tappets as described in paragraph (2). With these models, however, no flats are provided on the tappet, the stem automatically being prevented from rotating by means of small fillets. Be most careful when making an adjustment not to impose a strain upon these fillets.

With regard to correct valve clearances, on the 1936-8 Model G14 give 0·004 in. and 0·008 in. for inlet and exhaust valves respectively. In the case of the 1939 Model G14 the correct clearances are 0·006 in. for both valves.

(5) **O.H. Rocker Adjustment (1939 O.H.V. Model C11).** This model has direct-acting push-rods with no tappets and the valve

clearance adjustment comprises an adjuster screw on the push-rod end of each overhead rocker, as may be seen in Fig. 32. To check the valve clearances (which should be done with a *cold* engine), first put the piston at T.D.C. with both valves closed (page 49) and then remove the rocker-box cover by taking out the central fixing screw. Now insert a feeler gauge of the correct size between each rocker arm and the valve stem as illustrated. If an adjustment is needed, slacken lock-nut *B* with a spanner and with another small spanner applied to the flats on the adjuster screw

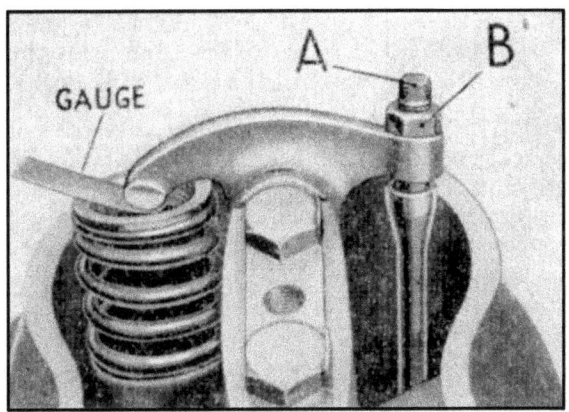

FIG. 32. O.H. ROCKER ADJUSTMENT ON 1939 O.H.V. MODEL C11
The feeler gauge should just pass between the valve stem and the end of the rocker arm on this 250 c.c. coil ignition model

A, turn the screw left or right as required to correct the valve clearance. Finally re-tighten the lock-nut *B* against the rocker arm (while holding *A*) and again re-check the clearance.

The correct inlet and exhaust valve clearances for the O.H.V. Model C11 are 0·003 in. and 0·003 in. respectively.

(6) O.H. Rocker Adjustment (All 1936-8 O.H.V. Twins, 1936 O.H.V. Models R4, R19). An overhead rocker adjustment is also provided on these machines and clearances should be checked with a *cold* engine, with the piston at T.D.C. with both valves fully closed (page 49). Insert the feeler gauge in the manner shown in Fig. 32. In the case of the inlet valve only, the valve and rocker arm are enclosed by a cover and this must be removed by taking out the two fixing screws (Fig. 33). Adjust if necessary by loosening lock-nut *A* and turning the adjuster screw *B* by means of a spanner applied to its squared end until the correct clearance is obtained. Re-tighten lock-nut and re-check the valve clearances.

On all 1936-8 O.H.V. Twins (498, 748 c.c.) a clearance of 0·002 in. should be given for both inlet and exhaust valves. This applies also to the 1936 348 c.c. De Luxe O.H.V. Models R4, R19.

(7) Tappet Adjustment (1937-8 O.H.V. Models M19, M22-M24). On these machines the tappet adjustment should be made with the engine *cold*, as described in section (2) on page 51. When making the adjustment, however, it is best to hold the tappet head and turn the tappet stem by means of the flats *C* (Fig. 29). The adjustment in all cases should be such that the tappet can be freely rotated between the thumb and finger. Just perceptible up and down movement should also be present.

(8) O.H. Rocker Adjustment (All 1936 O.H.V. Singles With " Sump " Oil Tanks). Put the piston at T.D.C. with both valves closed (page 49) and check the clearances with a feeler gauge when the engine is *cold*. To adjust, remove the rocker-box cover by releasing the spring clip (Fig. 34), loosen the lock-nut *A* and turn with a spanner the square end of each adjuster screw *B* until the clearance is rectified. Finally re-tighten the lock-nut and re-check the clearance.

The correct inlet and exhaust valve clearances for the 1936 "sump" models (Q8, R5, R17, R20, Q7, Q21) are 0·003 in. and 0·003 in. respectively.

(9) O.H. Rocker Adjustment (1936 O.H.V. Models X0, B2, B18). These lightweight models with mechanical pump lubrication have an overhead rocker adjustment identical to that given in section (8) and the above instructions apply. On these engines, however, the rocker-box cover is removed by unscrewing two knurled nuts. With the engine *cold* set both valve clearances to 0·003 in.

Exhaust Valve Lifter Adjustment. As has been mentioned on page 49, it is important before checking valve clearances to see that there is a little backlash in the exhaust valve lifter. It is also of vital importance to maintain this backlash whenever the engine is running, otherwise incomplete seating of the exhaust valve will cause not only loss of compression during the compression strokes, but also burning of the exhaust valve during the firing strokes, accompanied probably by intermittent banging in the exhaust system. Never use the valve lifter for controlling speed.

If an examination reveals that pressure on the valve lifter lever

Fig. 33. O.H. Rocker Adjustment Provided on All 1936-8 O.H.V. Twins

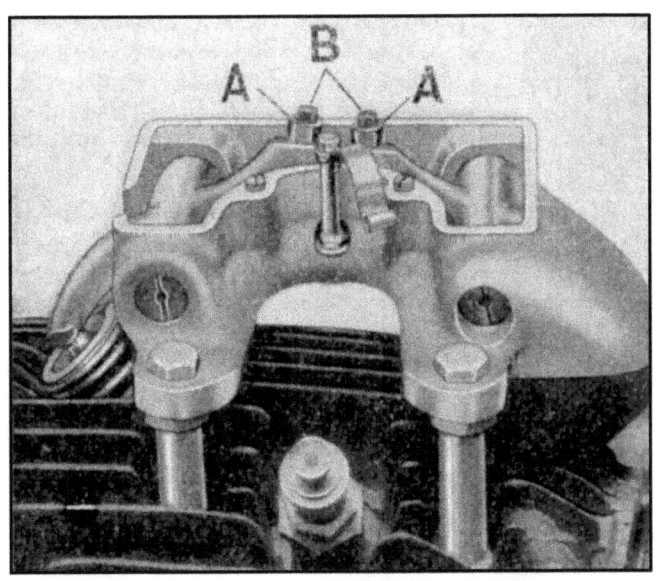

Fig. 34. O.H. Rocker Adjustment on 1936 O.H.V. Singles
This applies to engines with "C" type lubrication system (see page 19). 1936 "Empire Star" models have push-rod return springs fitted inside the push-rod covers

immediately actuates the overhead rocker or tappet, as the case may be, the cable adjuster on the off-side of the rocker-box or at the front of the cylinder, on O.H.V. and S.V. engines respectively, should be adjusted until the requisite degree of backlash is obtained (about $\frac{1}{16}$ in. to $\frac{1}{8}$ in.).

To Take Up End Play in O.H. Rockers. On certain 1936-9 O.H.V. engines, the rocker end play may be removed by the addition of special shims of 0·005 in. and 0·010 in. thickness. The latter can be supplied by the B.S.A. Spares Department.

THE IGNITION SYSTEM

The majority of motor-cycle roadside breakdowns are due to some fault in the ignition system. Such faults, however, usually develop through neglect on the rider's part to give that little maintenance and overhauling attention which is needed. All 1936-9 models except 1936 Model XO, 1939 Models C10, C11 have "Magdyno" ignition. Models C10, C11 have coil ignition, the battery supplying current for both lighting and ignition. Model XO has "Maglita" equipment.

Care of the Sparking Plug. Occasionally clean the sparking plug with petrol and scrape the electrode points lightly with a sharp pocket-knife, afterwards checking the gap between them, which should be 0·015-0·018 in. with "Magdyno" magneto, and coil ignition.*

Fig. 35. Lodge H14 Three-point Plug

Always adjust by bending the earth point, not the central electrode. The reach of the sparking plug is also of importance. The sparking plug should be inspected frequently. It is susceptible to oiling-up, especially during the running-in period and after decarbonizing or reboring.

An excellent gadget for quick plug cleaning consists of a metal reservoir containing petrol and steel wires. The plug is screwed into this and then vigorously shaken until clean. However, at considerable intervals it is wise to dismantle the plug and clean it thoroughly, which is not really possible without removing the

* When using non-sports plugs on earlier engines it is advisable to maintain the gap at about 0·020 in.

OVERHAULING

insulated electrode of the plug from the body. When dismantling, unscrew the gland nut with a plug dismantling tool or with a box spanner. On no account squeeze the body in a vice. All metal parts should be scraped with a knife and then rinsed in petrol. Do not scrape the insulation, but if coated with oil or soot, wash in petrol or paraffin. Next remove carbon deposits with fairly coarse emery cloth and again wash in petrol or paraffin. After cleaning the components, polish the electrode points with some fine emery cloth and reassemble, taking care not to overtighten the gland nut and to see that there is no grit between the insulator and metal body. Also make sure that the internal washer is correctly seated so as to give a gas-tight joint. Smear some thin oil on this washer. Finally check the gap, examine the copper washer, and clean the threads.

Always Fit a Good Plug. It is absolutely essential in order to obtain maximum performance and cool running always to fit a really good plug. This policy also is the cheapest in the long run. Three excellent plugs are the Champion, Lodge, and the K.L.G. If you have not a waterproof plug terminal, you should obtain one as this avoids the risk of shorting and misfiring in wet weather. A gauge can be obtained from the plug manufacturers.

All recent B.S.A. engines are fitted with 14 mm. plugs as standard but 18 mm. plugs are specified on some earlier models. Suitable 18 mm. plugs for S.V. machines are the Lodge C3, the K.L.G. M50. If 14 mm. plugs are required on S.V. engines, fit a Lodge C14, Champion L-10, or a K.L.G. F50. On O.H.V. engines taking 18 mm. plugs, fit a Lodge H1 or a K.L.G. M60 or M80. In the case of O.H.V. engines requiring 14 mm. plugs, use a Lodge H14, Champion L-10S, or else a K.L.G. F70. An excellent racing Lodge plug (14 mm. size) is the Lodge R42. For racing, however, always consult the plug manufacturers first.

Care of "Magdyno" (Ignition Unit). Little attention is required (for maintenance of dynamo unit, see page 34), and if any serious trouble arises it is best to return the instrument to the makers for attention. Never remove the armature.

The contacts of the contact-breaker (Figs. 36, 37) should be examined on a new machine after the first 100 miles, again after 300 miles and subsequently about every 3000 miles, and, if the "break," with the contacts full open, should be considerably more or less than will just hold a 0·010 in.-0·012 in. blade of a feeler gauge they should be adjusted. Too great a gap will advance the timing. A special magneto spanner is provided, which includes a gauge for checking the "break." It is unnecessary to remove the contact-breaker to make this adjustment. All that is necessary is to revolve the engine until the contacts are wide open, slacken the nut securing the fixed contact

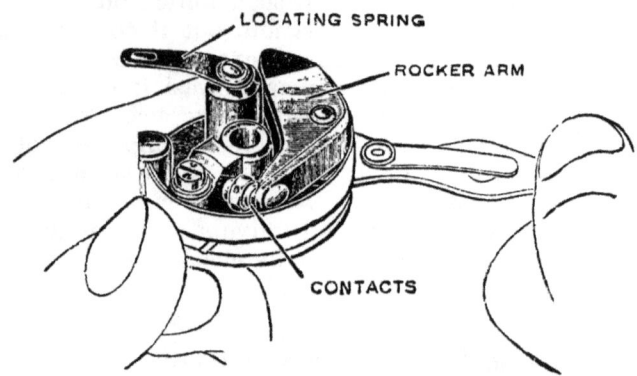

Fig. 36. Showing "Magdyno" Ring Cam Contact-breaker and Method of Removing the Rocker-arm (see also Fig. 20)

screw and then adjust the screw to which the fixed contact is fitted until the correct gap is obtained with the aid of a feeler gauge.

The contacts only need attention at long intervals, and the

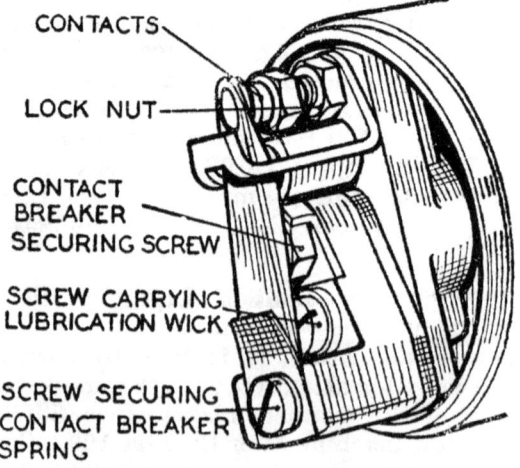

Fig. 37. The Lucas Face Cam Type Contact-breaker Used on Most Recent "Magdynos"

reader should not interfere unnecessarily with them. The greatest care must be exercised. Always keep the contact-breaker scrupulously clean. On examination after a big mileage the contacts

OVERHAULING

may be found to have irregular and dull surfaces due to burning (especially if the contacts have not been kept clean and properly adjusted), and if such is found to be the case it is necessary to polish them up, otherwise misfiring and rapid deterioration of the contacts will inevitably follow. To polish up the contacts, use a fine carborundum stone or emery cloth (do not use a file) and with the contact-breaker and rocker arm removed polish the contacts until all pitting is removed and the contact surfaces are bright all over. Be careful to keep the surfaces "square" as well as uniform. To remove the contact-breaker and rocker arm from a ring cam contact-breaker on a Lucas "Magdyno," proceed as follows.

Withdraw the contact-breaker from its housing by unscrewing the hexagon-headed screw (Fig. 20) in the centre by means of the magneto spanner. The complete contact-breaker can then be pulled off the tapered end of the armature to which it is keyed. Next push aside the locating spring and with a magneto spanner prise off the rocker arm from its bearings as shown in Fig. 36. After polishing the contacts wipe away all traces of dirt and metal dust with a rag moistened in petrol. When refitting the contact-breaker be very careful to see that it engages the key-way on the end of the armature properly, otherwise the ignition timing may be upset.

To remove the spring arm carrying the moving contact on a face cam type contact-breaker (Fig. 37), it is only necessary to withdraw the securing screw. It is important when replacing the arm to make sure that the small backing spring is replaced immediately under the securing screw and spring washer, with the bent part facing outwards.

Occasionally remove the H.T. pick-up. Wipe the moulding then with a dry cloth, and examine the carbon brush. It should work freely in its guide and not be unduly worn. When examining the brush avoid stretching the pick-up brush spring unduly, or a new one will be required. Renew both the brush and spring if they are in questionable condition. Also occasionally clean the slip ring track and flanges by holding a soft cloth wrapped around a pencil through the pick-up hole and slowly revolving the engine. Little attention is required in regard to lubrication of the armature bearings and this is referred to on page 25.

The Lucas Distributor Unit (Coil Ignition). At 6000 miles remove the moulded cover and inspect the contact-breaker contacts which are shown in Fig. 38. The contacts must be kept quite clean and free from grease or oil. If burned or blackened, polish the contacts as in the case of the "Magdyno" with fine carborundum stone or emery cloth and afterwards wipe quite clean with a petrol-moistened rag. If much attention is necessary to the contacts it is best to remove the rocker arm from its housing as follows: unscrew the nut securing the end of the contact-breaker spring and remove the nut together with the spring washer. Remove the metal bush and lift the contact-breaker lever off its bearing; also remove the rocker arm from its housing. Finally, after polishing and cleaning the contacts, refit the rocker arm, contact-breaker lever, metal bush and spring washer. Afterwards replace and tighten up the nut.

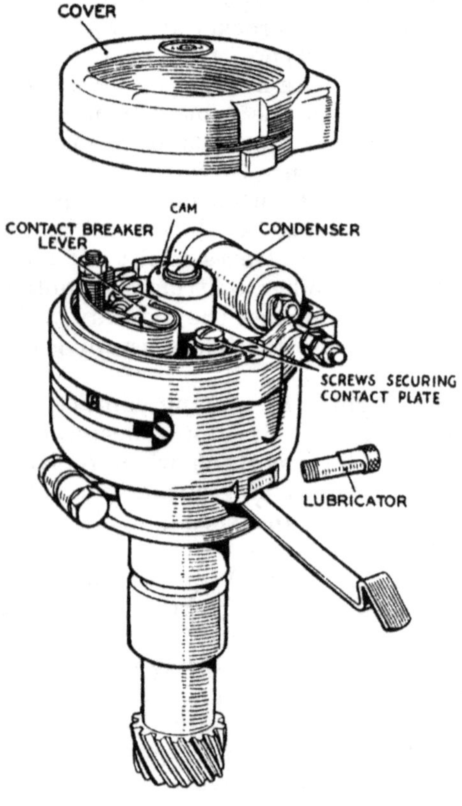

The contact-breaker gap should be maintained at 10 to 12 thousandths of an inch, and to test the gap, which requires adjustment only at long intervals, slowly revolve the engine by hand until the contacts are wide open. Then insert between the contacts the gauge provided on the ignition lever screwdriver, which should just slide in. If the gap is considerably too large or too small, adjust by opening the contacts fully and then slackening the locking screws until the plate carrying the stationary contact can just be moved. Now adjust the position of the plate until the correct gap at the contacts is obtained. Afterwards the locking screws must be re-tightened and the gap again checked.

FIG. 38. THE LUCAS CONTACT-BREAKER (COIL IGNITION MODELS)

The Battery. On the coil ignition 1939 Models C10, C11, it is important to keep the battery in good condition owing to the dual demands made upon it for lighting and ignition (see page 36).

Attention to Coil. The Lucas coil used on coil ignition models requires no attention whatever other than occasional cleaning

OVERHAULING

of the exterior, especially the space between the terminals. See that the connexions at the terminals are kept tight, and the wiring is in good condition.

What the Warning Lamp is For. The ignition warning lamp, which is combined with the ammeter in the headlamp on the coil ignition models, gives a red light when the engine is stationary and the ignition is switched on. This red light warns the rider that he should switch off the ignition to prevent current discharging from the battery in the event of the contacts at the contact-breaker being closed. The warning lamp goes out immediately the engine runs fast enough to cause the dynamo to charge, but it may continue to show when the engine is idling slowly. Should the bulb burn out, running of the engine will not be affected, but the bulb should be replaced as soon as possible. Always fit a Lucas 2·5 volt (0·2 amp.) bulb.

The ignition key (which is detachable) is incorporated in the centre of the headlamp lighting switch. To switch on, push the key in and turn *clockwise*. A coil ignition wiring diagram is given on page 41.

Symptoms of a Faulty Condenser. The condenser, which is connected in parallel with the contact-breaker circuit and is designed to prevent arcing at the contacts at the moment of the "break," rarely gives trouble and symptoms of such trouble are unmistakable. If heavy sparking occurs between the contacts and the latter rapidly become pitted and blackened, suspect the condenser immediately.

The Ignition Timing Control. No adjustment for the automatic ignition advance mechanism fitted on Models C10, C11 is provided, but some lubrication is needed (see page 26). In the case of other models with hand control, keep the ignition fully advanced except for starting and when the engine is pulling slowly on full throttle (i.e. when hill climbing).

Testing a Plug. Lay the plug on the cylinder with h.t. lead attached and the terminal clear of the cylinder and note if a "fat" spark occurs on kicking over the engine.

"Magdyno" Chain Adjustment (1936 Models B1, B2, B18). These three lightweight machines are the only singles having chain-driven "Magdynos." Being completely enclosed, the chain seldom requires adjustment, but after a considerable mileage the chain cover should be removed and the tension of the chain examined. The total up and down movement at the centre of the chain in its tightest position should be about ½ in. To adjust, slacken the two nuts on the left-hand side of the base plate and move the unit until the correct tension is obtained. After re-tightening the nuts, again check the tension.

To Adjust " Magdyno " Chain (1936-9 986 c.c. Twins). The above remarks regarding chain tension apply, but in this case it is necessary after removing the chain cover to release the two bracket bolts below the "Magdyno" and then move the "Magdyno" as required to give the necessary $\frac{1}{2}$ in. up and down movement of the chain.

To Adjust Dynamo Chain (1938-9 Models C10, C11). Do not allow a total whip of less or more than $\frac{1}{2}$ in. To adjust the dynamo tension, slacken off the clip bolt and rotate the eccentrically mounted dynamo gently. To ensure a proper oil seal, it is essential to keep the dynamo pressed against the chain case.

IGNITION AND VALVE TIMING

Ignition Timing. Accurate ignition timing is extremely important. Many riders imagine that by advancing their timing they necessarily will get more speed. This is a fallacy, and it only throws unfair loads on the engine, spoiling its flexibility and, eventually, damaging it throughout. For all normal road uses, the spark settings given in the table on page 64 should be closely adhered to. Only for genuine racing purposes is it advisable to increase the spark advance beyond these limits, and even then undue spark advance should be avoided. It should always be remembered that should the timing be so far advanced that maximum explosion pressures are reached with the crank in true T.D.C. position, the big-end comes in for a terrific hammering for which it is not designed. If the "Magdyno" has been removed for any purpose or the drive disturbed, it will be necessary to re-time it, and to do this proceed as follows.

(1) All " Magdyno " Singles. Set the piston so that it is at the top of the compression stroke and as near the T.D.C. position as possible (see page 49). Verify that it is on the compression and not the exhaust stroke by noting whether both valves are fully closed with the normal clearances at the tappets or rockers, as the case may be. Now remove the "Magdyno" timing cover, or timing cover plug on 1936 engines with "sump" oil tanks. Next loosen the "Magdyno" pinion fixed on the tapered end of the armature. Probably the pinion is rather stiff, in which case a lever may be wedged tightly at the back of it after undoing the nut a couple of turns. Now direct a sharp tap on the pinion nut which should free the pinion from its taper. If it does not, employ an extractor. Then remove the sparking plug or dummy plug provided for the purpose on S.V. engines, check that the piston is still at T.D.C., and insert a pencil or piece of wire through the hole. Make a mark on the pencil or wire, and measure carefully, and place another mark ⅜ in. (or whatever the exact ignition advance is) above the first one. Rotate engine slowly backwards until the top mark occupies the place previously held by the bottom mark, the piston having obviously descended ⅜ in. as the case may be; then set the contact-breaker so that the points just commence to separate (about 0·002 in.) with the spark lever on *full advance*.

To find the exact point of break, place a thin piece of paper (such as cigarette paper) between the closed contacts and turn the armature forwards until the paper is just released, and no more, on pulling it gently. When first tightening the pinion nut, the "Magdyno" should be held from rotating by means of the contact-breaker until the taper of the pinion begins to "bite" on the armature spindle taper. Be most careful, however, not to hold the contact-breaker for final tightening, otherwise it may become damaged.

Having checked the ignition timing after tightening the pinion nut, check the gap at the contacts when fully open (page 57) before replacing the timing cover or (on certain 1936 singles) the timing cover plug. When replacing the timing cover and washer some jointing compound should be used at the joint to prevent oil leakage. The engine is now ready for starting up and testing.

(2) 1938-9 Coil Ignition (Models C10, C11). Set the piston at T.D.C. with both valves closed, as explained in section (1) and then, using a marked piece of wire as already referred to, rotate the engine *backwards* until it has descended a distance equal to the ignition advance given in the table on page 64. Now remove the distributor cap and rotate the spindle until there is about ⅜ in. between the opening position of the cam and the fibre heel. Next insert the distributor in its housing with the flat side of the body towards the *rear* of the motor-cycle. Push the distributor down on to its seating and observe that as the distributor gear meshes with the skew driving gear the distributor shaft turns slightly, so that the cam takes up a new position. Then rotate the distributor body slightly until the contact-breaker points are commencing to "break."* In this position finally tighten the external locking screw situated at the front. Afterwards check the gap at the contact-breaker with the contacts wide open (page 60).

* Note that when the engine is stationary the timing is automatically *fully retarded*, the normal position for timing the ignition.

BOOK OF THE B.S.A.

Ignition Timings for 1936-9 B.S.A. Engines

(The timings are given in measurements on the piston stroke before T.D.C., presuming the ignition is fully advanced)

Engine	Model	Advance Before T.D.C. (in.)	Engine	Model	Advance Before T.D.C. (in.)
1936			**1938**		
149 c.c. O.H.V.	X0	$\frac{5}{16}$	249 c.c S.V.	B20	$\frac{5}{16}$
249 c.c. S.V.	B1	$\frac{1}{4}$	249 c.c. O.H.V.	B21	$\frac{7}{16}$
249 c.c. O.H.V.	B2	$\frac{5}{16}$	249 c.c. O.H.V.	B22	$\frac{7}{16}$
249 c.c. O.H.V.	B18	$\frac{5}{16}$	348 c.c. S.V.	B23	$\frac{5}{16}$
348 c.c. O.H.V	R4	$\frac{1}{4}$	348 c.c. O.H.V.	B24	$\frac{7}{16}$
348 c.c. O.H.V.	R17	$\frac{5}{8}$	348 c.c. O.H.V.	B25	$\frac{7}{16}$
348 c.c. O.H.V.	R19	$\frac{1}{4}$	348 c.c. O.H.V.	B26	$\frac{7}{16}$
348 c.c. O.H.V.	R20	$\frac{5}{8}$	348 c.c. O.H.V.	M19	$\frac{7}{16}$
496 c.c. O.H.V.	Q21	$\frac{5}{8}$	496 c.c. O.H.V.	M20	$\frac{3}{8}$
496 c.c. O.H.V.	Q8	$\frac{5}{8}$	591 c.c. S.V.	M21	$\frac{3}{8}$
348 c.c. O.H.V.	R5	$\frac{5}{8}$	496 c.c. O.H.V.	M22	$\frac{3}{8}$
499 c.c. S.V.	W6	$\frac{7}{16}$	496 c.c. O.H.V.	M23	$\frac{3}{8}$
496 c.c. O.H.V.	Q7	$\frac{9}{16}$	496 c.c. O.H.V.	M24	$\frac{3}{8}$
498 c.c. O.H.V.	J12	$\frac{9}{16}$	748 c.c. O.H.V.	Y13	$\frac{9}{16}$
595 c.c. S.V.	M10	$\frac{9}{16}$	986 c.c. S.V.	G14	$\frac{9}{16}$
748 c.c. O.H.V.	Y13	$\frac{9}{16}$	**1939**		
986 c.c. S.V.	G14	$\frac{9}{16}$	249 c.c. S.V.	C10	$\frac{1}{32}$
1937			249 c.c. O.H.V.	C11	$\frac{1}{32}$
249 c.c. S.V.	B20	$\frac{5}{16}$	249 c.c. O.H.V.	B21	$\frac{5}{16}$
249 c.c. O.H.V.	B21	$\frac{7}{16}$	249 c.c. O.H.V.	B21*	$\frac{7}{16}$
249 c.c. O.H.V.	B22	$\frac{7}{16}$	348 c.c. S.V.	B23	$\frac{7}{16}$
348 c.c. S.V.	B23	$\frac{5}{16}$	348 c.c. O.H.V.	B23*	$\frac{5}{16}$
348 c.c. O.H.V.	B24	$\frac{7}{16}$	348 c.c. O.H.V.	B24	$\frac{7}{16}$
348 c.c. O.H.V.	B25	$\frac{7}{16}$	348 c.c. O.H.V.	B24†	$\frac{7}{16}$
348 c.c. O.H.V.	B26	$\frac{7}{16}$	348 c.c. O.H.V.	B25	$\frac{7}{16}$
348 c.c. O.H.V.	M19	$\frac{7}{16}$	348 c.c. O.H.V.	B26	$\frac{7}{16}$
496 c.c. S.V.	M20	$\frac{5}{16}$	348 c.c. O.H.V.	B26†	$\frac{7}{16}$
595 c.c. S.V.	M21	$\frac{5}{16}$	496 c.c. S.V.	M20	$\frac{3}{8}$
496 c.c. O.H.V.	M22	$\frac{3}{8}$	496 c.c. S.V.	M20*	$\frac{3}{8}$
496 c.c. O.H.V.	M23	$\frac{3}{8}$	591 c.c. S.V.	M21	$\frac{3}{8}$
748 c.c. O.H.V.	Y13	$\frac{9}{16}$	498 c.c. O.H.V.	M22	$\frac{3}{8}$
986 c.c. S.V.	G14	$\frac{9}{16}$	498 c.c. O.H.V.	M22†	$\frac{3}{8}$
			496 c.c. O.H.V.	M23	$\frac{3}{8}$
			496 c.c. O.H.V.	M23†	$\frac{3}{8}$
			496 c.c. O.H.V.	M24	$\frac{7}{16}$
			986 c.c. O.H.V.	G14	$\frac{9}{16}$

* These are De Luxe models.
† Two-port engines are fitted to these models.

(3) Twin-cylinder Models. The instructions given in paragraph (1) are applicable also to the 1936-9 498, 748, 986 c.c. Twins, but certain points should be noted. Always time a twin-cylinder engine on the *front* cylinder and see that the H.T. distributor leads are not mixed up. The 986 c.c. S.V. engines have chain-driven "Magdynos," but all the smaller O.H.V. engines have gear-driven "Magdynos." In order to re-time, this, of course, necessitates the removal of either the chain case cover or the timing cover plug respectively. Removal of the "Magdyno" sprocket

FIG. 39. SHOWING "MAGDYNO" DRIVING GEARS AND TIMING GEARS ON 1937-9 250, 350 C.C. ENGINES

Note the large diameter piston type tappets. The exhaust camwheel has been taken out. On the 1939 coil ignition models a single camwheel timing gear (Fig. 40) is used and on 1939 "Magdyno" models except B21, B23 an outrigger plate (Fig. 40) is fitted

may be effected in the same manner as removal of the pinion on gear-driven models. After re-timing the engine correctly (see page 64), securely tighten the pinion or sprocket nut and check the timing before replacing the plug in the timing cover or the chain cover, as the case may be. On chain-driven models ascertain when the chain cover is removed that chain tension is correct (see page 62). Finally check the gap at the contact-breaker with the contacts wide open (page 57). See that the gap is the same for *both* cams.

Valve Timing. The correct valve timings for the various B.S.A. engines have been determined by the manufacturers after much experiment and calculation and B.S.A. owners are not advised to alter the original timings. All B.S.A. timing gears are marked, so there is no excuse for incorrect valve timing!

Twin camwheel timing gears are used on all 1936-9 B.S.A. engines except the 1938-9 coil ignition Models C10, C11 and the 1936 Models R4, R19. The arrangement of the timing gears is

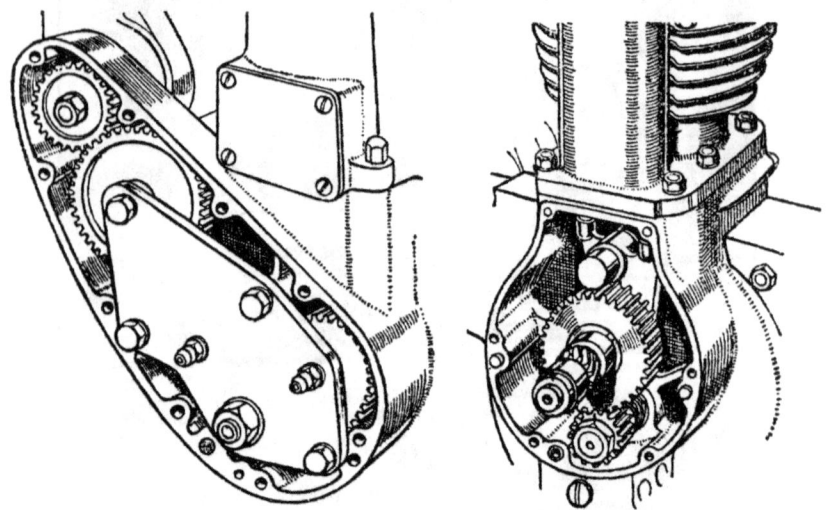

FIG. 40. SHOWING (LEFT) 500, 600 C.C. TIMING GEARS, AND (RIGHT) 250 C.C. TIMING GEARS USED ON COIL IGNITION MODELS

On all 1939 "M" type engines except Model M21 the timing gear spindles are supported by an outrigger plate as shown, the gears rotating on stationary spindles. On 1937-8 "M" type engines and the 1939 Model M21 the timing gear spindles rotate in bushes pressed into the timing cover.

(*From "The Motor Cycle"*)

shown in Figs. 39 and 40. The dash or dash and dot system of marking the engine pinion and camwheel(s) is employed. On all 1936-9 singles except Models C10, C11, R4, R19 the inlet camwheel should be meshed with the engine pinion so that a dash between two camwheel teeth registers with a dash on one of the engine pinion teeth. Similarly the exhaust camwheel should be meshed with the engine pinion so that a dot between two of the camwheel teeth registers with a dot on one of the engine pinion teeth. On most 1939 engines the camwheels are partly hidden by an outrigger plate (Fig. 40) bolted to bosses inside the timing case. This improves silence, and on removing the timing cover there is no risk of the timing gears being pulled away. On 1937-8 B20-B26 engines the "Magdyno" idler pinion is marked and it must be replaced so that the dot registers with the dot on the inlet camwheel, otherwise the operation of the crankcase breather will be affected.

In the case of the single camwheel timing gear used on the 1936 Models R4, R19 (see Fig. 10), the dot on the intermediate wheel should be meshed with the engine pinion so that the dots register, and then the camwheel should be meshed with the intermediate wheel so that the dash marks register. On the coil ignition Models

FIG 41. HOW THE TIMING GEARS ARE MARKED ON THE 1936-9 1000 C.C. ENGINES

This arrangement of the timing gears applies to all twin-cylinder engines

C10, C11 it is only necessary to mesh the camwheel with the engine pinion (Fig. 40) so that the dash marks register. Care must, however, be taken *before* removing the camwheel spindle always to raise the distributor, otherwise the distributor driving pinion may become damaged. To raise the distributor, release the external clip and raise the distributor up about ½ in.

The timing gears used on the 1936-9 986 c.c. Twins is shown in Fig. 41. To ensure the valve timing being correct it is only necessary to mesh the camwheels as indicated. On the 1936-8 496, 748 c.c. Twins the dot system of marking is used for the meshing of the engine pinion with the rear camwheel and the dash system for the meshing of the two camwheels.

To Dismantle Timing Gear (1937-9 498 c.c. Engines). By removal of the timing cover screws the cover itself may be removed by lightly tapping with a mallet the special projections formed on the cover for this purpose. The camwheels are housed partly in the cover and partly in the crankcase so that when the cover is withdrawn care should be taken to see that the cams do not fall out. The camwheels may then be withdrawn.

The outrigger bearing system was first introduced on the 1939 range and to remove the camwheels first remove the timing cover as above. This will expose a plate covering the cams. By undoing six set-screws this plate may be removed, thus allowing the camwheels to be withdrawn off the spindles.

DECARBONIZING

Decarbonize only when this is *necessary*, say on a B.S.A. O.H.V. engine every 2000-2500 miles and on a S.V. engine every 2500-3000 miles. Grind-in the valves *if necessary*. With an S.V. engine, however, it is usually sufficient to grind-in the valves every *alternate* decarbonizing. The piston should also be removed every alternate decarbonizing and the rings inspected. Decarbonizing is very simple, especially on S.V. engines, and it is not necessary to remove the cylinder during each "top overhaul" because most of the carbon deposits form on the piston crown, which is accessible on removing the cylinder head. The necessity for decarbonizing is indicated by a gradual falling off in power, a tendency for knocking (injurious to the engine) under slight provocation, and a "woolly" exhaust. The sparking plug also tends to become dirty very quickly.

Things You Need. You will need a jar of paraffin, some clean rags, some paper or a box on which to lay the parts (if no bench is available), a suitable scraper such as a screwdriver, some emery cloth, a tin of metal polish, and some engine oil. If you intend grinding-in the valves, you will also require a valve spring compressor, a valve grinding tool, and some coarse and fine grinding paste (such as Richford's). If the engine exterior is dirty, clean it thoroughly with rags and paraffin before commencing to dismantle.

Is Petrol Tank Removal Necessary? On all 1936-9 S.V. models it is quite unnecessary to disturb the petrol tank when decarbonizing, but on the 1939 O.H.V. engines (except "M" models) decarbonizing is greatly facilitated by complete removal of the tank from the frame. To do this, first undo the saddle nose bolt and after ascertaining that the petrol is turned off, disconnect the petrol pipe. Do not, however, drain the tank. Now proceed to remove the tank which is bolted at the rear to the top frame tube and at the front to the steering head lug. Be careful not to damage or lose the rubber insulators. See also page 46.

In the case of the 1939 "M" models complete removal of the

tank is not needed. Instead, free the tank from the top frame tube and steering head lug anchorage and then lift the tank and wedge it in a position which gives easy access to the rocker-box. Do not forget first of all to disconnect the petrol pipe after seeing that the petrol tap is turned off.

On all 1937-8 "B" and "M" models it is sufficient to lift the petrol tank (see above), but on 1937-9 250 c.c. and 1936 O.H.V. single and 1936-8 Twins the tank *need* not be touched. It should be mentioned, however, that many riders prefer always to remove the tank completely when decarbonizing, whether this is actually *necessary* or not.

(1) **Preliminary Dismantling (S.V. Singles).** Where it is intended to remove the detachable cylinder head only, detach the H.T. lead from the sparking plug and remove the latter. Also remove the engine steady arm (where fitted) which extends from the cylinder head to the saddle pillar lug.

If the cylinder barrel is to be removed as well as the cylinder head in order to grind-in the valves and remove the piston, disconnect the petrol pipe, remove the carburettor slides and needle by unscrewing the knurled lock-ring above the mixing chamber, tie them up out of the way, and then remove the carburettor by undoing the flange nuts. Detach the exhaust pipe and disconnect the exhaust valve lifter (where fitted) by first withdrawing the pin from the exhaust valve lifter cable fork end, when the valve lifter mechanism may be unscrewed as a unit from the wall of the valve chest. This applies to 1937-9 engines. On earlier engines disconnect the cable from the lever.

(2) **Preliminary Dismantling (S.V. Twins).** If the cylinder heads only are to come off for a "top overhaul," remove both h.t. leads from the sparking plugs and take out the latter. Where the cylinder barrels also are about to be removed, disconnect the petrol pipe, remove the carburettor slides and needle and tie them up out of the way. Next detach the carburettor from the inlet manifold by unscrewing the clip screw on the inlet manifold. Then remove the manifold itself and also both exhaust pipes. It is unnecessary to disconnect the exhaust valve lifter as this is situated between the cylinders. With regard to subsequent dismantling, deal with *one cylinder at a time*.

(3) **Preliminary Dismantling (O.H.V. Singles).** First of all deal with the petrol tank as described on page 68. Then detach the h.t. lead from the plug and unscrew the latter. Next remove the engine steady arm (where fitted) which extends from the rocker-box to the saddle pillar lug. Also disconnect the petrol pipe and remove the carburettor (on some machines the float chamber

needs detaching first) by withdrawing the slides and needle and then undoing the flange nuts (clip fixing on 1936 lightweights). The exhaust pipe(s) should now be removed and also on 1937-9 dry sump engines the external oil feed to the O.H. rocker spindles and the oil return pipe from the cylinder head to the crankcase. Finally before attempting to remove the rocker-box and cylinder head (dealt with in later paragraphs) the exhaust valve lifter should be disconnected in the following manner.

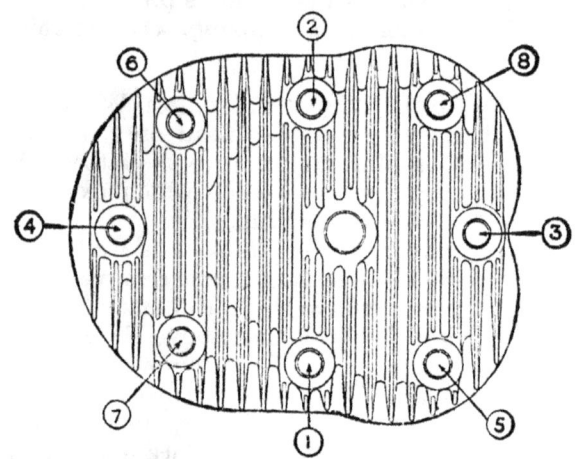

FIG. 42. ORDER OF TIGHTENING CYLINDER HEAD BOLTS (1936-9)
The above order applies to 249, 348, 986 c.c. engines. The bolts should be removed in the reverse order to that shown. On 496, 591 c.c. engines the order is similar but two extra bolts are included

On 1939 models turn the engine over so that the exhaust valve is wide open (exhaust tappet fully raised) and then detach the cable from the small lever on the cylinder head by withdrawing the pin from the fork end, and unscrew the cable adjuster from its anchorage. On 1937-8 engines open the exhaust valve fully and detach the small lever on the cylinder head by removing the fixing nut, and unscrew the cable from its anchorage. On 1936 models with the exhaust valve wide open disconnect the ball at the end of the cable from the lifter lever on the rocker-box and screw out the cable and adjuster.

(4) Preliminary Dismantling (O.H.V. Twins). Disconnect the h.t. leads, remove both plugs, also the petrol pipe and both exhaust pipes. Then remove the carburettor slides and needle and tie them up out of the way. Undo the two ring nuts on the inlet manifold and detach the manifold complete *with* carburettor. Drain the oil tank.

To Remove Cylinder Head (S.V. Models).

Having "cleared the deck" as indicated in section (1) or (2), proceed to remove the cylinder head bolts. When doing this, be careful to unscrew the bolts *evenly* and, starting from one bolt, to work round in a criss-cross order (see Fig. 42). After removing all the bolts which hold the head(s) to the barrel(s), lift the former off, exposing the piston(s) and valves. If the joint is stiff, replace the plug, and turn the engine over against full compression; this should loosen the joint, but if it fails to do so, gently prise the head upwards with a suitable tool wedged between the head and barrel. Put the piston at T.D.C. if it is not already in this position, so as to prevent dirt from entering the highly polished cylinder bore, or better still, cover the top of the cylinder barrel with a rag. The cylinder head gasket should be examined and if there are any signs of blowing or damage it should be renewed.

To Remove Cylinder Head (All 1939 O.H.V. Singles Except Models M24, C11).

Remove carburettor, exhaust pipe(s), plug, etc., as described in section (3) and with the petrol tank removed on "B" models or raised on "M" models (see page 68), proceed to remove the rocker-box. First of all remove the rocker-box cover which is held in position by twelve small bolts and four large bolts in line. The last-mentioned pass through the rocker-box and secure it to the cylinder head. To remove the cover, unscrew all the bolts and remove them with the exception of the rearmost one which at this juncture cannot be removed. Now swing to one side the rocker-box cover and take out the remaining bolts which hold the rocker-box to the cylinder head; two are located between the rocker spindles and two outside the rocker-box adjacent to the valve springs.

Next remove the two nuts at the base of the push-rod casing; this will permit of the rocker-box being taken off complete with its cover, push-rods and push-rod casing. Unless it is desirable to renew the oil sealing washer, the gland nut at the top of the push-rod casing should not be disturbed. Having removed the rocker-box assembly, unscrew diagonally the four bolts which clamp the cylinder head and barrel to the crankcase. The spanner must be applied to the hexagonal portion just below the lowest cylinder fin. The cylinder head joint (metal to metal) may now be broken by sharply tapping the underside of the head near the exhaust port with a mallet. Lift the head off and be most careful with the machined joint faces (see page 80). Cover the top of the cylinder with a rag until you commence to decarbonize. A point to note is that *under no circumstances* should an attempt be made to remove the cylinder bolt anchorage sleeves which are screwed into the crankcase.

To Remove Cylinder Head (1939 Model M24). In the case of the 496 c.c. "Gold Star" the push-rod casing is integral with the cylinder barrel and this necessitates a dismantling procedure slightly different from that described above for the other 1939 O.H.V. singles. First remove the petrol tank (see page 68). Next remove carburettor, exhaust pipe, plug, etc.—see section (3) on page 69. Then remove the rocker-box cover and rocker-box. Having done this, draw the push-rods upwards out of the casing and release the four cylinder bolts from the crankcase, followed by the three remaining bolts whose heads are visible on the under side of the bottom fin on the cylinder barrel. Also remove the two short bolts on the sides of the push-rod housing. If difficulty is experienced in releasing the rearmost bolt, lift the cylinder assembly from the crankcase, when a spanner may readily be applied. Now break the cylinder head joint as described in the previous paragraph. Note also the previous remarks about the four anchorage sleeves.

To Remove Cylinder Head (1939 Model C11). This 249 c.c. O.H.V. engine differs from other B.S.A. engines considerably. After removing the parts which hinder dismantling, described in section (3), undo the central screw which secures the rocker-box cover and take off the latter. Then remove the seven nuts which hold the head on to the barrel. These nuts are inverted and are located between the second and third cylinder barrel fins. The cylinder head may now be gently prised off the barrel, or if the joint is stiff, tapped off with a mallet applied near the exhaust port. Be careful with the copper-asbestos washer and if there are signs of "blowing," renew. The push-rods which are crossed on this engine may be freed from the rocker ball pins and withdrawn as soon as the cylinder head is raised slightly.

To Remove Cylinder Head (All 1937-8 O.H.V. Singles). Lift the petrol tank* (page 68), remove the carburettor, plug, exhaust pipe(s), etc., as described in section (3) on page 69. Then on 1938 models unscrew the gland nut at the top of the push-rod casing and the two nuts on the flange at its base. Now lift the push-rods off the tappets by means of a screwdriver inserted through the tappet cover and allow the push-rods to drop down to the crankcase.

Unscrew the four cylinder holding-down bolts at the hexagon portion near the cylinder bottom fins, and by sharply tapping the underside of the cylinder head with a mallet or similar tool,

---

* On the 250 c.c. O.H.V. models the rocker-box and cylinder head may be detached without disturbing the petrol tank.

OVERHAULING

the head can be freed from the barrel. Lift the petrol tank and withdraw the cylinder head complete with rocker-box and cover. The push-rods, casing and gasket may now be removed. To detach the rocker-box (Fig. 43) from the cylinder head on "M" models, first remove the cover by undoing the twelve screws and then unscrew the six attachment bolts. On "B" models to detach the rocker-box from the cylinder head, first remove the cover by undoing the six screws and four bolts and then unscrew the two bolts situated between the rockers.

Fig. 43. 1937-8 Rocker-box with Cover Removed
Fitted to many engines of 250 c.c. to 500 c.c. Note the pressure oil feed to the hollow rocker shafts

When removing the four cylinder bolts leave the anchorage sleeves alone. They are screwed into the crankcase and must *not* be touched on any occasion.

In the case of the 1938 Model M24 ("Gold Star") the push-rod casing is integral with the cylinder barrel. To remove the cylinder head, release the four cylinder bolts, lift the push-rods off the tappets with a screwdriver inserted through the tappet cover and allow the push-rods to drop down into the crankcase. Now break the cylinder head joint, swing the head through 180 degrees and lift off the cylinder barrel.

To Remove Cylinder Head (1936 O.H.V. Singles Except Models B3, R4, R19). After initial dismantling (page 69) remove the inlet valve lubricator union bolt, the rocker-box cover and then the four rocker-box bolts. Next release the nuts at the bottom of the push-rod tubes. Then withdraw the rocker-box, push-rods and push-rod tubes towards the right-hand side of the machine, the upper portions first. Undo the four cylinder head nuts, tap the head lightly and draw it carefully off the barrel studs, removing it from the left-hand side of the machine.

To Remove Cylinder Head (1936 Models B3, R4, R19). After initial dismantling (page 69), drain the oil tank and remove the inlet valve lubricator union bolt at the valve end. Remove the four rocker-box bolts. Release the nuts at the bottom of the push-rod tube. Then withdraw the rocker-box, push-rods, and push-rod tube, towards the right-hand side of the machine, the upper portions first. The four nuts holding the cylinder head can then be undone. Tap the head lightly and draw it off the studs, removing it from the left-hand side of the machine.

To Remove Cylinder Head (1936-8 O.H.V. Twins). Preliminary stripping down should be carried out as indicated in paragraph (4) on page 70. Then remove the union bolt of the inlet valve lubricator pipe at the cylinder head and unscrew the packing gland nut at the top of each push-rod cover tube. Remove the rocker-box lubricator pipe union bolt and remove the rocker-box itself by taking out the four fixing bolts. Each cylinder head is secured by the four rocker-box supports and their removal enables the head to be lifted off the cylinder barrel studs.

When decarbonizing twin-cylinder engines it is preferable to deal with one cylinder at a time as this avoids the risk of mixing up the components. Decarbonizing is required less often on Twins than on the singles and therefore it is well worth removing the cylinder barrels and pistons. The valves should also be inspected at the same time and if necessary ground-in.

To Remove Cylinder Barrel. This is straightforward once the cylinder head has been removed. On S.V. engines remove the four nuts holding the cylinder base flange to the crankcase and also on some 1937-9 S.V. singles the set-screw or nut located *inside* the tappet chest. On 1937-9 O.H.V. engines where four elongated bolts screw into the crankcase sleeves and retain both the cylinder barrel and head, it is presumed that the bolts are already removed (see page 73). On other O.H.V. engines remove the four nuts which hold the cylinder barrel flange to the crankcase. Whether nuts or bolts are fitted, remember to unscrew them evenly in a diagonal order.

Now lift the cylinder up and forwards into the front angle

OVERHAULING

(rear angle for back cylinder of a Twin) of the frame and then turn the engine forward with the kick-starter until the piston emerges from the mouth of the barrel. Be very careful when holding the barrel with the right hand not to impose any strain on the piston or connecting-rod, and as soon as the piston sees daylight steady it to prevent its skirt falling sharply against the connecting-rod or crankcase. Finally cover up the top of the crankcase with a rag or cloth to prevent any dirt or foreign bodies getting inside. If the cylinder base washer has been damaged during cylinder removal, a new one must be fitted before reassembly.

Piston Removal. The piston used on B.S.A. engines is of aluminium alloy with two compression rings and one special scraper ring (Fig. 44). It is held to the small-end of the connecting-rod by a fully floating gudgeon-pin. To prevent scoring on 1936 single-cylinder engines the gudgeon-pins have soft end caps, but all subsequent Singles and all 1936-9 Twins have the usual pair of circlips. Where end caps are fitted, to remove the piston it is only necessary to push or tap the gudgeon-pin from one side. This should be done immediately after removing the cylinder while the piston is still warm. Where wire circlips are provided, remove one with a small screwdriver or tang end of a ground file. Then push or tap the gudgeon-pin out from the opposite side. A circlip must fit snugly into its groove in the piston boss because if it works loose, it may ruin the cylinder. If in any doubt about the condition of a circlip, renew it with a genuine B.S.A. circlip. On removing the gudgeon-pin, make a slight nick on one end to ensure correct replacement.

Mark the Piston. A piston laps out the cylinder in which it reciprocates in a certain manner depending upon piston thrust, lubrication and other factors, and it is most inadvisable to replace it in any except its original position on the connecting-rod; that is to say, it should not be replaced back to front or vice versa. Therefore, unless the piston has some distinguishing characteristic it is always advisable to mark it to ensure its correct replacement. Perhaps the best plan is to scratch an "F" on the inside to indicate which is the front. Be careful not to interchange the pistons on a twin-cylinder engine, and always remember that a piston should be handled with care as it is readily distorted or cracked.

Examining and Removing Piston Rings. The piston rings are the main-guard of the compression. They must, therefore, be full of spring, free in their grooves, and set with their slots opposite to each other (i.e. at 120° in the case of the three-ring piston which is fitted on all 1936-9 B.S.A. engines). If all three rings are bright all the way round, they are obviously being polished against the cylinder walls, and are perfect, and should be left alone. If, on the other hand, they are dull or stained at some points, they are not in proper contact with the walls of the cylinder. Perhaps they are stuck in their grooves with burnt oil, and will function properly if the grooves are cleaned. If vertically loose in their grooves or have brown patches, the rings must be renewed. Piston rings are of cast-iron and, being of very small section, must be handled very, very carefully. If not, they will certainly be broken. They cannot safely be opened out wider than will allow them to slip over the crown of the piston. Therefore, to put them on or remove them requires the insertion of small strips of metal, about $\frac{1}{2}$ in. wide by 2 in. long, which are placed in the manner illustrated by Fig. 44. Be most careful to note the order in which the rings are removed so as to ensure proper replacement. When fitting piston rings, thoroughly clean the grooves into which they fit, as any deposit left at the back of new rings forces them out and makes them too tight a fit. Paraffin usually loosens stuck piston rings. Piston rings are made to very accurate dimensions, and it is very bad practice to attempt to "fit" oversize or undersize rings unless you know exactly what you are doing. Lapping-in oversize piston rings is a skilful job, and unless the slot sizes are exactly right, the rings will not function well, and may even produce an engine "seizure." Therefore, always use piston rings supplied by B.S.A. Cycles, Ltd. Special austenitic compression rings must be used on engines with linered cylinders (1938-9 B21, M20, M21, M24), but they must not be used in conjunction with cylinders made of cast-iron. The correct gap at the slots for all rings is 0·003 in. to 0·004 in. per inch of cylinder diameter. To test the gap, push the ring into the cylinder bore with the piston until it is quite "square" and about mid-way up the stroke. Then with a feeler gauge of the right size check the gap.

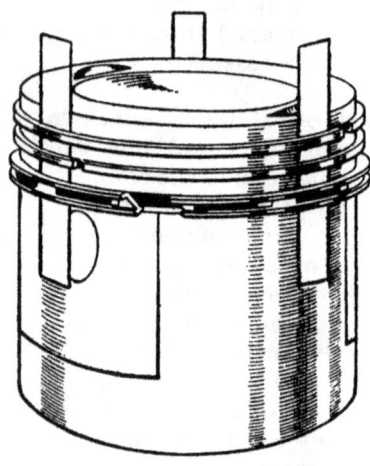

FIG. 44. SAFE METHOD OF REMOVING PISTON RINGS
This method (see text) should also be used for refitting rings. Note the slotted scraper oil control ring below the compression rings on the B.S.A. piston

Generally speaking, when the gap exceeds 0·012 in. it is time to fit a new ring. Keep an eye on the ends of the three rings. If they are bright, this indicates that the gap is insufficient; if, on the other hand, they are thick with carbon the gap is probably excessive. If the gap is too small, clamp the ring between two wood blocks in a vice and file one of the diagonal ends slightly. If a new ring is found to be a tight fit in its groove, rub down one side of the ring on a piece of carborundum paper laid on a sheet of plate glass. A special scraper ring is fitted on B.S.A. pistons (Fig. 44) and be careful to replace this exactly as removed and with the scraper edge correctly positioned. A final word of advice: if the piston is doing its job well, leave the rings alone. Good compression indicates that all is well.

Removing the Carbon. Thoroughness in decarbonizing well repays the labour expended. To clean the cylinder-head, the best

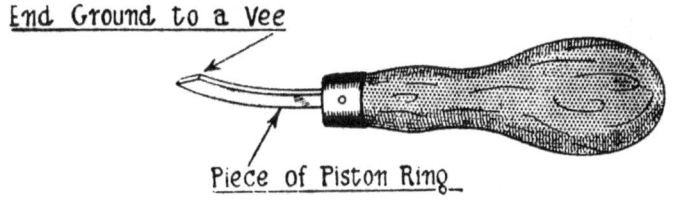

FIG. 45. A USEFUL TOOL FOR CLEANING PISTON RING GROOVES

tool is a blunt knife or screwdriver, with which the carbon can be scraped and chipped from the head, great care being taken to see that the combustion chamber is not deeply scratched.

Remove all traces of carbon from the interior surfaces and do not forget the sparking plug hole and the exhaust port(s). Carbon forms less readily on a smooth surface and therefore it is a good plan to polish a cast-iron type head with fine emery cloth, but do this before removing the valves, and afterwards clean all abrasive particles away with petrol. Also scrape all carbon from the valve heads. Be very careful with an aluminium-alloy head.

In the case of an O.H.V. head with metal to metal joint, care should be taken that the ground joint of the head is not damaged. A good method of holding the head whilst decarbonizing is to fit a hexagon steel bar screwed at one end (Fig. 46) into the plug hole. The cylinder head may then be held in a vice by means of the steel bar. If such a bar is not available, an old sparking plug makes a useful substitute. This will facilitate the operation considerably.

With the comparatively soft aluminium alloy piston be careful when removing the carbon. Do not use emery cloth, the carbon being removed by means of a blunt knife or screwdriver alone and the surface afterwards wiped with a rag damped in petrol. Make no attempt to remove carbon from the skirt or the lands between the rings. A little carbon is usually deposited on the *inside* of the piston. When the piston is removed, this should be removed. The screwdriver can be used for this till all carbon is scraped off. Take care not to let screwdriver shank bump unnecessarily against the piston skirt, or the latter may crack. Examine ring grooves for carbon. Should any be present, scrape out with a tool such as that shown in Fig. 45. The rings should also be scraped at the back. Wash piston and rings thoroughly in clean petrol. Refit rings by slipping them over the piston, using the three strips previously described, if necessary.

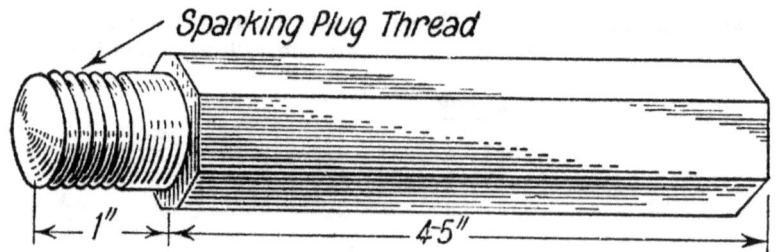

Fig. 46. A Hexagon Steel Bar Turned and Threaded at one End to Hold the Cylinder Head when Decarbonizing

To Remove the Valves. As has already been mentioned (page 68), the valves should be removed and inspected every *alternate* decarbonizing and *if necessary* ground-in. On S.V. engines it is possible to remove the valves with the cylinder in position, but it is much better to take off the barrel. On O.H.V. engines the valves are, of course, housed in the detachable head. Split collets are used for valve spring anchorage on all B.S.A. engines except 986 c.c. engines, which have flat cotters, and if any difficulty is experienced in compressing the valve springs, you should obtain and use a B.S.A. valve spring compressor which may be purchased from any B.S.A. dealer.

Should no valve spring compressor be available, the following method can be employed for compressing the valve springs on S.V. or O.H.V. engines. Place some hard packing under the valve heads (O.H.V.); place cylinder or cylinder head so that the valves or packing are flush with the bench. Then press down on the valve spring collars with a spanner or other suitable tool until the spring is compressed enough to enable the split collets to be removed. The valve can then be drawn out.

How to Grind-in. Use a screwdriver for S.V. engines and the valve holder supplied in the tool-kit for O.H.V. engines. To grind-in a valve hold the cylinder or cylinder head firmly on a bench or in a vice (see page 77), and after cleaning both the valve seat and valve, smear with a piece of rag or the finger tip a thin film of grinding paste (coarse first if dealing with an exhaust valve) on the valve face and replace the valve in its guide minus the valve spring. Before inserting it, however, it is a good plan on S.V. engines to insert a small spring between the valve head and valve guide to avoid the necessity of frequently lifting the valve off its seat by hand in order to turn it round, which is necessary to avoid the formation of grooves or rings on the valve face while grinding-in. Never interchange the valves.

When grinding-in, a steady pressure on the grinding tool is required and care must be taken not to rock the valve, particularly if the valve guide is somewhat worn. Rotate the valve about *a third of a turn* in one direction and then an equal amount in the opposite direction, pausing about every half-dozen oscillations to raise the valve from its seat and turn it one-third to a quarter of a revolution. Cease grinding-in when no "cut" can be felt (and the valve begins to "sing") and put some more paste on the bevelled edge of the valve face if after cleaning the valve in paraffin some pitting is still visible. Continue grinding-in until both the valve face and seat have a matt surface over a considerable depth (line contact is not sufficient) and there are no pit marks left on wiping the paste off. Do not continue grinding-in after a good seating has been effected, because excessive grinding-in eventually leads to the valves becoming "pocketed," which causes a considerable decline in power output. Badly pitted valves or seats should be dealt with at the B.S.A. works. After grinding-in the inlet and exhaust valves wipe both the valves and their seats thoroughly clean with a paraffin- or petrol-soaked rag to ensure that there is absolutely no trace of any abrasive left. Examine the valve guides for wear and renew if much play exists, otherwise slow-running will become difficult. Also renew valve springs if weak.

Refitting Valves. After grinding-in the valves you should reassemble them in the cylinder head. Smear the valve stems with oil and replace them in their guides. Then refit the valve springs and collars, being careful not to mix up the upper and lower collars. Next compress each valve spring (see opposite); and refit the split collet or cotter, making certain that it beds down properly. The application of a little grease to the lower part of the valve stem facilitates reassembly on O.H.V. engines, as this enables the split collet to stick on the valve stem.

After Reassembly. On O.H.V. engines it is an excellent plan to test the seats by pouring some petrol into the ports and watching for leakage past the valves. Not the slightest sign of moisture should creep past the valves until after a considerable time has elapsed. If some petrol quickly gets past the valves, it is sure proof that the valves have not been sufficiently ground-in and the remedy is (horrible thought!), remove and continue grinding-in. The ultimate test of good valve seating is engine compression.

Grinding-in Cylinder Head and Barrel Faces. If either faces (with a metal to metal joint) have been damaged in removal of the head, it will be necessary to regrind these in, in the same manner as one would a valve. The holes from which the bolts have been taken should first be filled with grease, so that the grinding compound is kept out of the threads. The head and barrel should then be rubbed together, similar to the grinding-in of valves. A good joint may be made between the head and the barrel by smearing a little Hermatite on the faces.

Refitting Piston and Cylinder. This should be done in the reverse order of dismantling after pouring a little oil into the crankcase. Smear both the piston and inside of the cylinder with engine oil and refit the piston the correct way round (page 75) on the connecting-rod, pushing the gudgeon-pin, which should also be oiled, home from the side where the circlip (where fitted) has been removed. Fit a new circlip on this side (unless you are sure the old one is perfect) and see that the butt end beds down properly in the piston boss slot and is fully expanded. Remember that if a circlip "goes west" with the engine running you may have to put your hand in your pocket for a new piston and cylinder. Also see that the cylinder barrel spigot and mouth of the crankcase are scrupulously clean and that the base washer is replaced. On later engines warm piston before fitting the pin.

To replace the cylinder put the crank slightly past B.D.C. with tappets right down, space the rings properly (see page 75), hold the cylinder in the angle of the frame over the piston with one hand and offer the piston up to it with the other, squeezing the rings (without upsetting the position of the gaps) together until the complete piston enters the cylinder. Avoid putting any side strain on either the piston or connecting-rod. After seeing that the spigot beds down on the crankcase squarely and closely, tighten up the cylinder nuts (when fitted) finger-tight first and then securely with a spanner *a quarter* of a turn at a time diagonally Even tightening is important, otherwise there is some risk of distorting the cylinder flange and preventing its bedding down properly on the crankcase. On S.V. engines do not forget the nut inside the valve chest. On twin-cylinder engines deal with each cylinder in turn.

OVERHAULING

Final Reassembly (All S.V. Engines). Clean the faces of the cylinder barrel and cylinder head and then replace the cylinder gasket; if it shows signs of leakage (indicated by black patches), fit a new one. Now carefully lower the cylinder head on to the barrel, insert the cylinder head bolts and tighten them down evenly *a quarter of a turn* at a time in the correct order (see Fig. 42). These bolts will require re-tightening after about 250 miles. Check the tappet clearances carefully, re-connect the exhaust valve lifter, and replace the tappet cover. Now fit the exhaust pipe and carburettor. When replacing the latter, be careful not to damage the needle while replacing the slides. Also see that the carburettor is firmly bolted to the cylinder. On twin-cylinder engines (where most assembly operations have to be duplicated) replace the inlet manifold before attaching the carburettor with the clip fixing. The manifold and carburettor joints must be absolutely air-tight. Finally replace the sparking plug(s) and h.t. lead(s). If the petrol tank has been removed, replace it.

Final Reassembly (1939 O.H.V. Models Except C11). Having replaced the cylinder barrel (page 80), refit the cylinder head after cleaning the joint faces and smearing the latter with a little jointing compound. Now screw up the four cylinder bolts lightly at first and then tighten down with a spanner *a quarter of a turn at a time*. The bolts must be tightened in a diagonal order and will require re-tightening again after 250 miles have been covered.

Next fit the rocker-box into position, complete with push-rods and push-rod casing. Fit the rearmost rocker-box fixing bolt and also the rocker-box cover loosely in position before attempting to replace any of the remaining rocker-box bolts. Place the push-rods in position between the tappets and the rocker arms by inserting the fingers through the tappet inspection cover, and bolt the rocker-box to the cylinder head and the push-rod casing to the crankcase. Refit the exhaust valve lifter and exhaust pipe(s). Fit the oil return pipe from the cylinder head to the crankcase and replenish the valve spring housings in the cylinder head with engine oil to the level determined by the oil return pipe. Replace the rocker-box cover and the external oil feed pipe to the rocker spindles.

Refit the Amal carburettor, taking special care not to injure the needle when replacing the slides. Replace the petrol tank on "B" models, or retighten the tank nuts on "M" models, and see that the rubber pads are replaced in the correct order. Also refit the petrol pipe. Clean the plug (page 56), replace it and adjust the tappet clearances (page 49).

Final Reassembly (1939 Model C11). After refitting the cylinder barrel (page 80), replace the cylinder head gasket. If this is damaged or shows signs of leakage (indicated by black patches), a new one should be fitted. Before fastening the cylinder head to the barrel replace the push-rods, making certain that the cup in the top end fits correctly with the rocker ball pin, and that the lower end rests in the cup formed in the cam rocker. *Note that the push-rods are crossed* and they must not be fitted in a parallel position. Now tighten the head firmly in position and refit the exhaust valve lifter. Before replacing the rocker-box cover, check the tappet clearances and adjust in accordance with the instructions given on page 52.

The carburettor should now be replaced and care should be taken not to damage the needle when replacing the slide. Refit the petrol pipe. Before replacing the sparking plug, it should be dismantled and cleaned in accordance with the instructions given on page 56. Finally replace the exhaust pipe and the petrol tank.

Final Reassembly (1937-8 O.H.V. Models). Proceed as follows, after refitting the cylinder barrel (page 80). Where a gasket is not fitted, smear a little jointing compound on the joint faces. Then place the cylinder head complete with rocker-box and exhaust valve lifter on the barrel and fasten the whole assembly to the crankcase by screwing up the four cylinder holding down bolts into the head. Make certain that the barrel is positioned correctly. Gradually tighten the bolts *a quarter of a turn* at a time. Re-tighten these bolts after about 250 miles.

Now turn the engine until the piston is at top dead centre on the compression stroke and replace the push-rod cover and push-rods, followed by the carburettor, sparking plug and exhaust pipe(s).

When replacing the carburettor examine the gasket, and if damaged in any way fit a new one of the same type and material. Check the tappet clearance and adjust if necessary (page 51). Replenish the rocker-box with engine oil to the level determined by the oil return pipe. Finally bolt down the petrol tank.

Final Reassembly (1936 O.H.V. Singles and 1936-8 O.H.V. Twins). Refitting of the cylinder barrel(s) has been dealt with on page 80. Where a cylinder head gasket is not fitted, smear some jointing compound on the joint faces. Then replace the cylinder head(s) and tighten them down evenly (see Fig. 42). Now rotate the engine gently until the tappets are right down and the piston is at T.D.C. on the compression stroke. Refit the rocker-box(es) push-rods and cover tube(s) and make sure that the tops of the vapour tubes spring into their seatings beneath the box(es). Check the valve clearances (page 53) and adjust if necessary.

OVERHAULING

On O.H.V. singles reconnect the exhaust valve lifter. Now refit the rocker-box cover(s), carburettor (with manifold on O.H.V. Twins), sparking plug(s) and exhaust pipe(s). Finally replace the petrol tank if this has been removed.

CARE OF TRANSMISSION (See Publishers Note - Page 96)

Little attention is needed to ensure smooth running of the transmission which comprises the gearbox (see page 95), the clutch, and the chains. Lubrication has been dealt with in Chapter II and the advice given should be carefully noted.

Attention to Foot Gear Change (Except 1939 Models C10, C11). Ordinarily the only attention (apart from lubrication) that the mechanism is likely to need is the very occasional replacement of a broken spring. A set of spare springs should always be carried by the rider in case of emergency. In the event of spring breakage, remove the outer gearbox cover and release the pedal from the splined shaft by slackening the pinch-bolt. Then slide the pedal off the shaft and remove the circlip. Now detach the clutch cable and undo the gearbox cover nuts, four of which are situated at the rear of the casing. Draw off the outer cover complete with kick-starter, leaving the gear change mechanism in position. This may be withdrawn complete after releasing the central spindle nut at the rear of the casing. Having done this, the broken spring may be removed and the replacement spring fitted by pressing its eyes over the anchoring pegs, using a small pair of pliers. All components (see Fig. 47) should be carefully inspected and if wear of parts is noticed, replacements should be made as necessary. The various parts should be cleaned and oiled before reassembly. It should be noted that the pedal shaft is splined to allow of the pedal being fitted in a position to suit individual requirements.

Foot Gear Change (1939 Models C10, C11). These two models have a slightly different gearbox design to the other models and the replacement of a broken pawl spring is the only attention likely to be required. To replace a spring, remove the outer cover and put the gears in the *neutral position*, disconnect the clutch cable and remove the kick-starter crank after withdrawing its cotter pin. Remove the spring-loaded plunger, which locates the selector mechanism, from the base of the inner cover near the front of the box. Leave the gear-change pedal in position, and remove the retaining screws from the cover; carefully remove it complete with foot change mechanism.

Next remove the broken spring and fix the new spring by

pressing its eyes over the anchoring pegs with the aid of a pair of pliers.

When replacing the cover, make certain that the spring-loaded

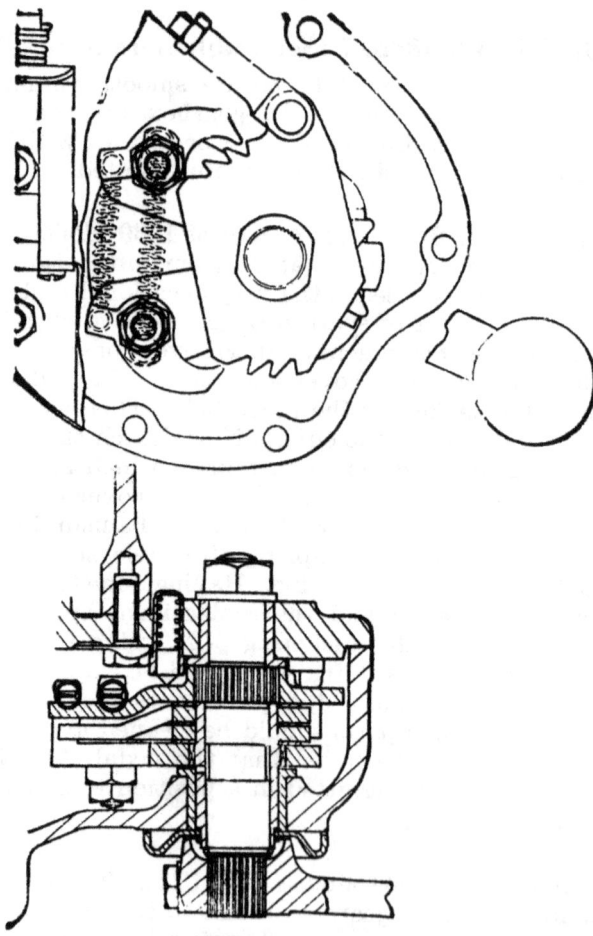

FIG. 47. SHOWING DETAILS OF THE B.S.A. FOOT GEAR CHANGE
This applies to all 1936-9 models (except 1939 Models C10 C11) without hand control

plunger, screwed in from the base of the inner cover, registers with the neutral gear groove in the selector plate. This is most important and the gear change will not function correctly if it is not assembled as indicated. The groove is the third one as measured from the front end of the gearbox.

OVERHAULING 85

The gear-change pedal may be placed on a different set of splines if required.

To Adjust Hand Gear Change (1936-9 Singles Except 1936 Model M10). If a considerable movement has been made in the position of the gearbox it will be necessary to readjust the gear control rod.

The adjusting piece is at the upper end of the rod. Disconnect

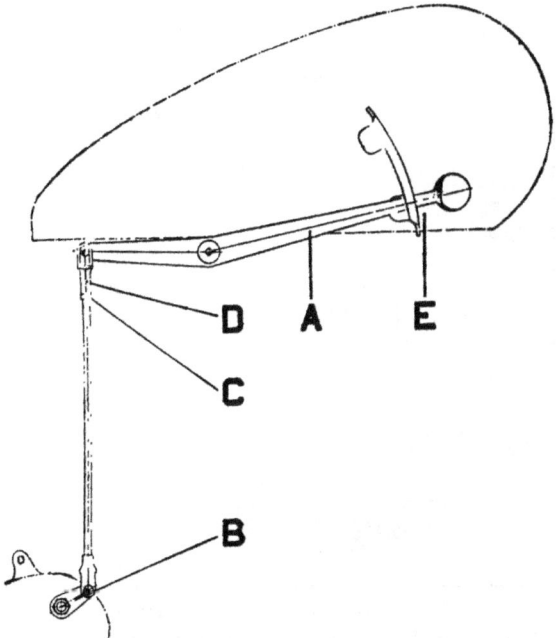

FIG. 48. ADJUSTMENT OF HAND GEAR CHANGE
This adjustment applies to all 1937-9 single-cylinder models

the rod from the operating lever by removing the screw, and then move lever *B* (Fig. 48) towards the rear (front on 1936 Models R4, R19) of the machine until the spring plunger inside the gearbox can be felt to have registered with its recess. Now move lever *B* foward one notch to give the neutral position. Set the operating lever *A* in neutral and adjust the sleeve *D*, after loosening the lock-nut *C*, until the screw can be replaced without altering the positions of *B* or *A*, and tighten nut *C*. When lever *A* is moved into 1st gear position, there should be a little clearance between the end of the slot and the lever. When moving the gear lever into the quadrant notches it should be possible to feel the action of the gearbox spring-loaded plunger.

To Adjust Hand Gear Change (1936 Model M10 and 1936-9 Twins). An adjustment is required after moving the gearbox to re-tension the primary chain. To effect this the lever *B* (Fig. 49) should be moved towards rear of machine until the spring plunger inside the gearbox can be felt to have registered with its recess. Now move lever *B* forward one notch to give the neutral position. The nuts *C* should now be slackened from sleeve *D*,

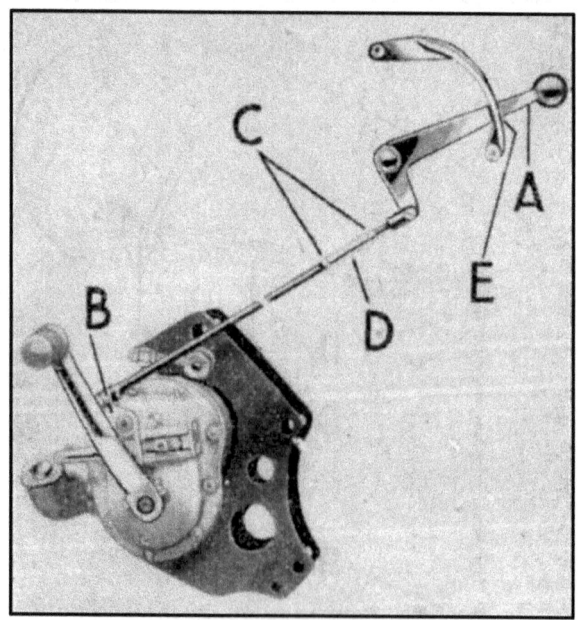

FIG. 49. ADJUSTMENT OF HAND GEAR CHANGE
This adjustment applies to all twin-cylinder models and also the 1936 S.V. single, Model M10

bearing in mind that the lower one has a left-hand thread. Sleeve *D* should now be moved until operating lever *A* is just in the neutral position. Then tighten nuts *C*. When lever *A* is moved into first gear position there should be a little clearance between the end of the slot and the lever.

When moving the gear lever in its quadrant it should be possible to feel the action of the spring-loaded plunger in the gearbox.

Clutch Adjustment. Multi-spring clutches have been specified on most B.S.A. models from 1937 onwards, but prior to 1937 the single spring type was predominant. Three means of adjustment are provided on the multi-spring clutch and adjustment should always be maintained such that there is no pressure on the

OVERHAULING

clutch push-rod when the handlebar lever is released. To be on the safe side, allow at least $\frac{1}{16}$ in. backlash in the cable. This applies to all clutches. To adjust the multi-spring clutch, slacken the lock-nut J (Fig. 50) after (on single-cylinder models) sliding the rubber protector up the control arm. Then make the necessary adjustment by means of the grub-screw E. Further adjustment can if necessary be made by means of the knurled thumb-nut G.

After a considerable mileage there may be a tendency to clutch

FIG. 50. ADJUSTMENT OF CLUTCH CONTROL

On single-cylinder models the operating arm is upright and its base is surrounded by a rubber protector. Above is shown the control on the 1939 S.V. Twin. Note the lubricator H

slip in spite of the above adjustments being correct. In this case it will be necessary to increase the spring pressure. Adjustment of the pressure is provided for except on the 1936 "Empire Stars" and the 1937 Models M20-M23. To adjust on single-cylinder models with multi-spring clutches, slacken the lock-nuts on the clutch outer plate (Fig. 18) and screw up the adjuster nuts on the bolts. While doing this be exceedingly careful to tighten all the nuts *the same amount*. Finally re-tighten the lock-nuts. The normal spring pressure adjustment is such that the lock-nuts are *flush* with the bolt ends. In the case of the 1936-7 models mentioned above which have no adjustment, the ring-nut on the mainshaft must always be kept firmly tightened.

To increase the spring pressure on 748, 986 c.c. twin-cylinder models, remove the clutch cover and unscrew the two large lock-nuts on the end of the main shaft. Then to increase the spring pressure, turn the ring-nut behind *clockwise*. To increase the spring pressure on 1936 Models J12, R17, R20, W6, Q7, Q21, remove the clutch cover and screw up the nut on the main shaft.

Dismantling Clutch. After a big mileage or if clutch slip occurs due to dirty or oily plates, dismantle the clutch and scour the plates with a stiff brush and petrol. To dismantle the multi-spring clutch on most single-cylinder models, remove the spring adjusters and spring cups, and draw the plates off. Be sure to replace them in the correct order. In the case of 1936-9 Twins and the 1936 Model M10 to dismantle, the nuts of the main shaft must be removed. On reassembly, screw two $\frac{1}{4}$ in. diameter × 26 T.P.I. screws through the clutch outer plate into the spring box plate behind it. This will compress the springs to enable the nuts to get a start on the thread. On 1936 single-spring clutches a special tool is available to compress the spring when reassembling. In the event of it being necessary to remove the clutch centre, a special B.S.A. extractor tool is obtainable.

The Cush Drive. The spring tension on 1936 models may be adjusted if necessary by means of the two ring-nuts holding the spring.

To Re-tension Primary Chain. Being totally enclosed, this seldom requires re-tensioning, but from time to time the tension should be checked by inserting the fingers through the inspection cover on the chain case. On a few 1936-9 models no inspection cover is fitted and in this case the outer half of the chain case must be removed. To re-tension the chain, slacken the gearbox fixing bolts or nuts (variously located on different models) and then with the adjuster move the gearbox backwards or forwards until the chain has about $\frac{1}{2}$ in. freedom up and down at a point mid-way between the sprockets, with the chain in its tautest position. After making the adjustment, re-tighten the gearbox fixing bolts or nuts; if the machine concerned has hand gear change, also check the gear control adjustment (page 85) and the rear chain.

To Re-tension Secondary Chain. The secondary chain, which has cam wheel adjustment, requires periodical re-tensioning. To do this, first slacken off the rear brake rod. Then loosen the spindle nuts and on models with a quickly-detachable wheel the knock-out spindle. On 1937-9 "M" models also slacken the chain adjuster situated between the off-side rear fork ends (Fig. 51).

Turn the spindle on the near-side with a spanner applied to the spindle flats until correct chain tension is obtained. This should be such that the chain has $\frac{3}{4}$ in. total up and down movement at the chain centre with the chain in its tautest position. See that the cams (cam on some models) are hard against the stops. Now on 1937-9 "M" models screw the off-side chain adjuster in or out, as the case may be, until the wheel is correctly aligned in the frame, using for this purpose the special alignment gauge supplied in the tool-kit (Fig. 51), or a straight edge.

Tighten the near-side nut first and then the off-side nut or

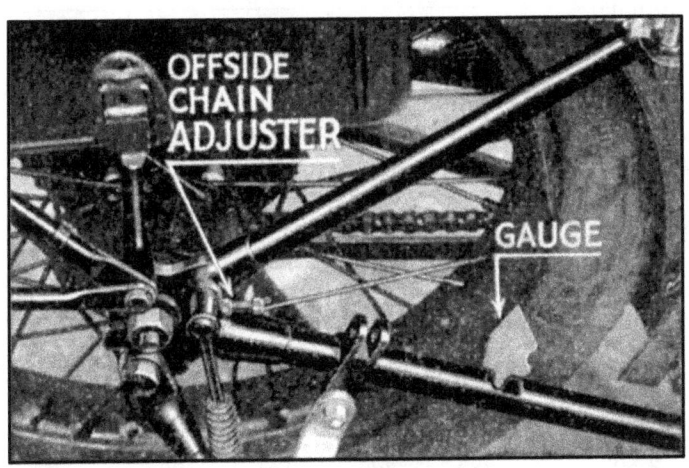

FIG. 51. REAR CHAIN ADJUSTER AND WHEEL ALIGNMENT GAUGE
These are fitted to the 1938-9 "M" models. On taking delivery of a new machine the owner should note which of the three gauge dimensions (marked 1, 2, 3) applies to his machine and use this only

knock-out spindle, as the case may be. Finally check the alignment of the wheel (already checked on "M" models) and adjust the rear brake (page 94). If occasion is had to remove a chain, see that it is replaced with the open end of the spring link facing *away from* the direction of motion. The cleaning of chains is dealt with on page 31.

TYRES, WHEELS, AND BRAKES

To Obtain Good Tyre Mileage. Always maintain the correct tyre pressures and keep the wheels in alignment. Avoid fierce acceleration, violent braking and stunt cornering. Handle the clutch gently, remove flints which bed into the cover, and keep oil or paraffin from getting on the treads.

Maintain Correct Tyre Pressures. Over-inflation causes vibration, strains the cover, and favours a tendency for concussion bursts; under-inflation produces a tendency for tyre creep, rolling, instability of steering, and cracking of the cover. All of these things are objectionable and you should therefore always run with the tyres inflated to the correct pressures and check the pressures weekly with a pressure gauge. The table below, reproduced by courtesy of the Dunlop Rubber Co., Ltd., indicates the

Nominal Tyre Section (Inches)	Inflation Pressures—lb. per sq. in.					
	16	18	20	24	28	32
	Load per Tyre—lb.					
2·375	120	140	160	185	210	240
2·50	120	140	160	185	210	240
2·75	140	160	180	210	250	280
3·00	160	180	200	240	300	350
3·25	200	240	280	350	400	440
3·50	280	320	350	400	450	500
4·00	360	400	430	500	—	—

correct tyre pressures for standard Dunlop tyres fitted to various machines and forms a useful guide. The rider must be *seated*.

Since variations in tyre section, weight and weight distribution all affect the question of tyre inflation the author advises you to write to the B.S.A. Co. and obtain the *exact* tyre pressures for your own particular machine, or else determine the load per tyre by placing each wheel on a suitable weighbridge. It will be appreciated that in a handbook of this size it is impossible to state the exact pressures for all 1936-9 models, which number sixty-six all told! It should be noted that where a passenger is carried, this must be considered.

Mending Punctures. On models with quickly-detachable wheels a portion of the rear mudguard is hinged to facilitate rear wheel removal; on other models part of the rear guard is detachable. The hinged or detachable portion is held by the lower rear chain stays. To remove the detachable portion, first disconnect the tail lamp wire and unscrew the two bolts in the mudguard in front of the lifting handle (where fitted). Then by removing the other two nuts at the lower rear stays, the tail piece may be removed. Note that these nuts are shouldered and that they must be located properly in the slots in the rear stays when replacing the tail. Wheel removal is dealt with in a later paragraph.

When removing a cover with tyre levers, start near the valve and push the opposite side of the cover into the base of the rim. Test for a puncture by submerging the tube in water. Clean the tube with sand-paper and rub off all dust. Next select a suitable auto-vulcanizing patch such as the "Vulcafix" and remove its linen backing. If solution is *not* used, rub the prepared face of the patch with a cloth moistened in petrol and transfer the brown deposit on the cloth to the punctured area. Repeat this operation and allow the patch and transferred deposit to dry for one minute. If solution *is* used, apply it to the *tube only* and allow it to become "tacky." Now affix the patch to the tube, using slight pressure, particularly at the edges, and apply french chalk.

To Remove Quickly-detachable Wheel. Quickly-detachable rear wheels are fitted to a large number of 1936-9 models. In the case of twin-cylinder models both wheels are of the quickly-detachable type. The same method of removal applies to each wheel.

To remove the detachable wheel on all except the 1938-9 "M" models, with the box spanner provided in the tool-kit remove the three retaining bolts from the hub centre (Fig. 52). Then withdraw the spindle and also the distance piece between the hub and the off-side fork end. This will enable the wheel hub to be drawn to the right off the three driving pegs on the brake drum. The wheel may now be pulled clear towards the rear. On the 1936 498 c.c. Twin no small hub-retaining bolts are fitted.

On the 1938-9 "M" models to remove the detachable wheel, take out the three retaining bolts from the hub centre and then remove the nut on the off-side of the spindle and withdraw the spindle from the *opposite* side. The spindle is a push fit in the hub and on no account must a spanner be applied to the spindle head. Rotation is purposely prevented by locating the head in the hub centre. Remove the distance piece, draw the hub to the right until clear of the dogs and then pull the wheel away to the rear.

On both the above types of detachable wheel it is extremely important after replacing the wheel to screw up the three retaining bolts absolutely tight.

To Remove "Non-detachable" Wheels. This is perfectly straightforward. In the case of the front wheel, disconnect the front brake cable from the shoe operating lever, disconnect the speedometer drive (where fitted), undo the spindle nuts, and slide the wheel out. Most machines have a quick-release front brake attachment. To disconnect the brake cable, raise the knurled sleeve to its limit, rotate slightly to lock in position, and withdraw the cable from the fork end.

In the case of the rear wheel, remove or lift the detachable or

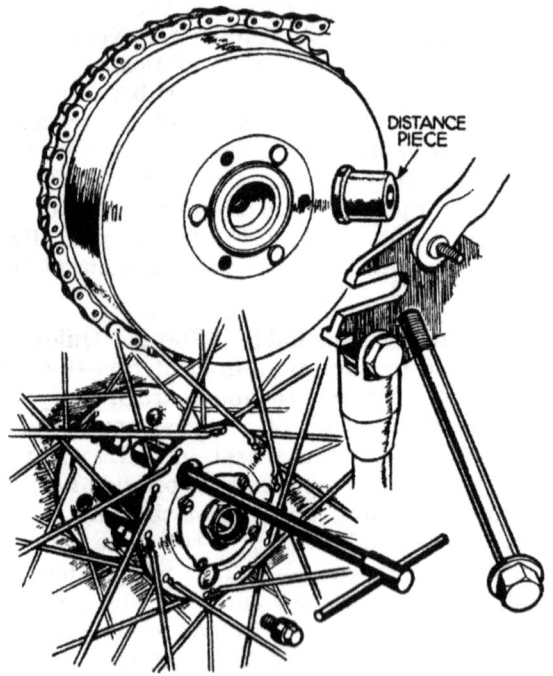

Fig. 52. Removal of Quickly-detachable Wheel (1936-7)
On 1938-9 "M" models a somewhat different design of detachable wheel is provided
(*From "The Motor Cycle"*)

hinged tail piece of the mudguard (page 91), disconnect the rear brake by removing the cam lever, uncouple the chain, remove the nut from the anchor plate chain stay connexion, loosen the spindle nuts and slide the wheel out backwards. Wheel removal does not affect the hub bearing adjustment.

Adjustment of Wheel Bearings. Some of the smaller B.S.A. models have cup and cone type ball bearings, but the majority have taper roller bearings. The wheels should frequently be tested for side play and the bearings adjusted if necessary, with the wheel out of the forks. It is essential in the case of both

OVERHAULING

ball and roller bearing hubs that the wheels should have just perceptible side play at the rim.

To adjust the front and rear hub bearings on machines with ball bearing hubs (also 1937-9 "B" models with roller bearings), and the front hub bearing on machines with roller bearing hubs, loosen the locknut on the off-side next to the hub and turn the adjusting sleeve on the inside of the lock-nut clockwise or anti-clockwise as required. Finally re-tighten the lock-nut. It is important when adjusting the bearing not to tighten up the adjuster sleeve excessively, otherwise the balls or rollers and their races may become damaged. To obtain the adjustment mentioned in the previous paragraph, the sleeve should be screwed in until all play disappears and then unscrewed about a third of a turn.

To adjust the rear bearing on machines with roller bearing hubs (also the rear bearing on 1936 Model M10 and the 1936-9 Twins), proceed as follows: release the lock-nut on the off-side, remove the locking plate carrying a peg* which engages the adjusting sleeve, and set the lock-ring in the nearest suitable position. Finally re-tighten the lock-nut.

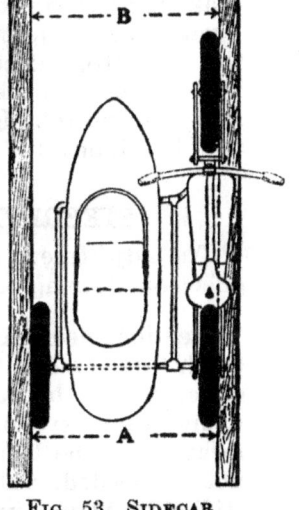

FIG. 53. SIDECAR ALIGNMENT

The distance B should be $\frac{1}{2}$ in. less than the distance A

Alignment of Wheels. In order to obtain maximum tyre life and good steering, the wheels must always be kept in perfect alignment. Moving the rear wheel in order to re-tension the secondary chain does not upset the alignment because all B.S.A. models except the 1938-9 "M" models have a twin cam adjustment of the wheel spindle, giving automatic alignment. On the "M" models mentioned a special alignment gauge (see page 89) is provided. If desired, it is easy to check the alignment of the motor-cycle wheels by placing a straight-edge or plank alongside the two wheels. It should, of course, touch the tyres at *four* points. Where a sidecar is fitted, the sidecar wheel should "toe-in" to the extent of $\frac{1}{2}$ in. (see Fig. 53). To adjust the front stay, release the clip at the sidecar end and move the stay to a suitable position in the spring bracket. Check the vertical alignment and if necessary adjust the telescopic seat pillar connexion until the

---

* On some machines the locking plate is perforated to take a peg pressed into the adjusting sleeve.

motor-cycle leans very slightly *outwards*. The nut securing the rear connexion (which has a spherical and spring washer) should be slacked back half a turn before fitting the split pin to enable the ball joint to function.

Brake Adjustment. For your own safety and that of others, keep the brakes in perfect condition. Adjustment of the rear brake is by means of a wing nut at the rear end of the brake rod. Front brake adjustment is by means of a knurled thumb nut on the cable stop, fitted to the front forks or front brake cover plate. If grease gets on the brake linings, remove the shoes and wash the linings in petrol. If the linings become smooth, roughen with a wire brush or a file. Do not adjust brakes too closely.

STEERING HEAD, FORKS, AND GEARBOX

The adjustment of the steering head and forks has a marked effect on steering and should be checked occasionally.

Steering Head Adjustment. To test for play in the steering head, first remove the weight from the front wheel by placing a suitable box beneath the engine. Then remove the steering damper and try and push and pull the front wheel towards and away from the head. If no "shake" exists an adjustment will not be needed, unless, of course, the head bearings are on the stiff side. To adjust the bearings, loosen the clip beneath the handlebars and gradually tighten the top adjuster nut until there is no perceptible "shake" and no friction. Do not overtighten, or the ball races may be injured. Finally tighten the clip nut and replace the steering damper knob.

Front Fork Adjustment. The need for adjustment is sometimes indicated by a creaking noise on turning the handlebars sharply and play can often be felt. The link bolts should always be kept done up sufficiently tight to eliminate side play. To adjust, slacken the lock-nuts on the near-side (and off-side, 1937-9 "B" models), screw up the bolts, and re-tighten the lock-nuts. Avoid making the adjustment too close. In order to be sure that binding is not taking place, slacken the shock-absorber. Afterwards adjust the shock-absorber to prevent bouncing on wavy roads.

To Replace Fork Spring. Pack up the engine so as to remove the weight from the front wheel. Then remove the nut from the top of the spring. Next remove the link bolts and links. The spring is now clear of the frame and can be taken away after removing the pin and nut on the bottom fixing.

To detach the scrolls, grip the bolts firmly in a vice and punch

OVERHAULING

the extremity of the spring to wind it off. The spring on reassembly can be wound on to the scroll by hand.

The Four-speed Gearbox. This is of the constant mesh type and the gear trains are shown removed in Fig. 54. The gear reductions are obtained by transmitting the drive through the main-shaft and lay-shaft gears. The different gears are obtained by selection through the agency of dogs and splines, the dogs being moved by striking forks operated by the control shaft which is connected to the gear control lever. A spring-loaded plunger is incorporated

FIG. 54. ARRANGEMENT OF GEARS IN B.S.A. FOUR-SPEED GEARBOX

in the selector mechanism. The kick-starter mechanism is housed in the first or outer end cover, the gears being contained within the second cover.

To Expose Kick-starter Mechanism. The gearbox outer cover must be removed to gain access to the kick-starter mechanism. To do this, uncouple the clutch cable from the operating arm and the cable adjuster from the end cover. Release the gear change pedal from its splined shaft by slackening the pinch bolt and slide the pedal off the shaft, followed by the two circlips and selector disc.

Remove the cover fixing screws and also the nuts behind, and on the edge of, the gear change housing. The outer cover may now be drawn off, complete with kick-starter quadrant, leaving the gear-change mechanism in place.

PUBLISHERS NOTE

Additional Clutch & Gearbox Overhaul Information

Unfortunately, the information on clutch and gearbox overhaul contained in this manual is not as comprehensive as many owners may require. More detailed information can be found in **'The Book Of 1930's British Motorcycle Gearboxes and Clutches' ISBN 9781588501813.** This publication includes overhaul details for the 1932 and prior BSA models fitted with 3 and 4 speed medium and heavyweight gearboxes and light, medium and heavyweight clutch assemblies. Much of this data is applicable to the 1936-1939 models.

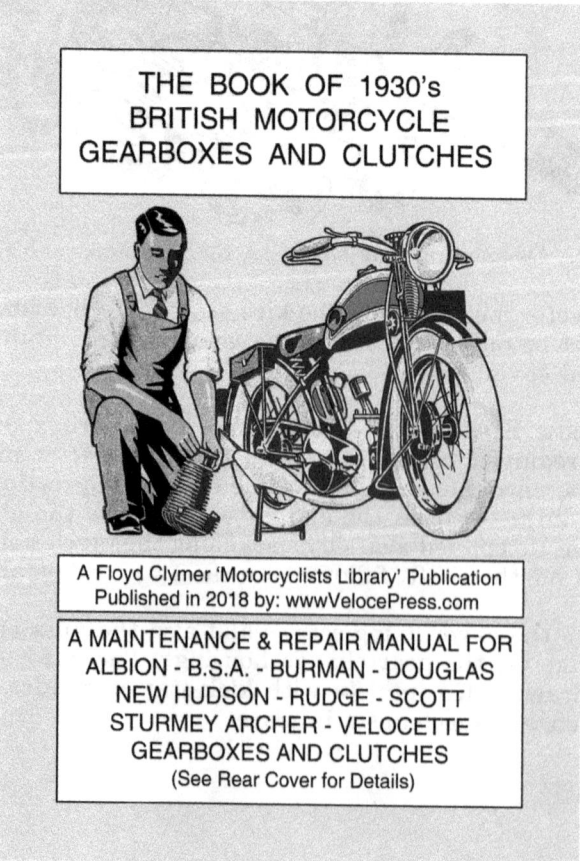

PUBLISHERS NOTE

Additional Engine Overhaul Information

Further details on engine overhaul and maintenance can be found in **'The Book Of 1930's British Motorcycle Engines'** **ISBN 9781588501912.** This publication includes supplemental information for the 1932 and prior 2.49HP, 3.49HP, 4.93HP, 5.57HP, 7.70HP and the 9.86HP Single and V-Twin OHV and SV engines many of which were still in use in the 1936-1939 models. This publication also includes a comprehensive 'Timing Chart' for the 1914-1931 engines.

VELOCEPRESS MANUALS - MOTORCYCLE

1930'S BRITISH MOTORCYCLE CARBS & ELEC COMPONENTS (BOOK OF)
1930'S BRITISH MOTORCYCLE ENGINES (OVERHAUL & MAINTENANCE)
1930'S BRITISH MOTORCYCLE GEARBOXES & CLUTCHES (BOOK OF)
AJS 1932-1948 SINGLES & TWINS 250cc THRU 1000cc (BOOK OF)
AJS 1945-1960 SINGLES 350cc & 500cc MODELS 16 & 18 (BOOK OF)
AJS 1955-1965 SINGLES 350cc & 500cc (BOOK OF)
ARIEL UP TO 1932 (BOOK OF)
ARIEL 1932-1939 PREWAR MODELS (BOOK OF)
ARIEL 1933-1951 (WORKSHOP MANUAL)
ARIEL 1939-1960 4 STROKE SINGLES (BOOK OF)
ARIEL 1958-1964 LEADER & ARROW (BOOK OF)
BMW R26 R27 (1956-1967) FACTORY WORKSHOP MANUAL
BMW R50 R50S R60 R69S (1955-1969) FACTORY WORKSHOP MANUAL
BRIDGESTONE 90 SERIES FACTORY WSM & PARTS CATALOGUE
BRIDGESTONE 175 SERIES FACTORY WSM & PARTS CATALOGUE
BSA BANTAM ALL MODELS FROM 1948 ONWARDS (BOOK OF)
BSA SINGLES & V-TWINS UP TO 1927 (BOOK OF)
BSA SINGLES & V-TWINS UP TO 1930 (BOOK OF)
BSA SINGLES & V-TWINS UP TO 1935 (BOOK OF)
BSA SINGLES & V-TWINS 1936-1939 (BOOK OF)
BSA OHV & SV SINGLES 250-600cc 1945-1959 (BOOK OF)
BSA OHV & SV SINGLES 250cc (ONLY) 1954-1970 (BOOK OF)
BSA OHV SINGLES 350 & 500cc 1955-1967 (BOOK OF)
BSA TWINS 1948-1962 (BOOK OF)
BSA TWINS 1962-1969 (SECOND BOOK OF)
CYCLEMOTOR (BOOK OF)
DOUGLAS 1929-1939 PREWAR ALL MODELS (BOOK OF)
DOUGLAS 1948-1957 POSTWAR ALL MODELS FACTORY SHOP MANUAL
DUCATI 160cc, 250cc & 350cc OHC MODELS FACTORY SHOP MANUAL
HONDA 50 ALL MODELS UP TO 1970 INC MONKEY & TRAIL (BOOK OF)
HONDA 90 ALL MODELS UP TO 1966 (BOOK OF)
HONDA 125-150cc TWINS C/CS/CB/CA FACTORY WORKSHOP MANUAL
HONDA 250-305 TWINS C/CS/CB FACTORY WORKSHOP MANUAL
HONDA C100 SUPER CUB FACTORY WORKSHOP MANUAL
HONDA C110 SPORT CUB 1962-1969 FACTORY WORKSHOP MANUAL
HONDA TWINS & SINGLES 50cc THRU 305cc 1960-1966 (BOOK OF)
HONDA TWINS ALL MODELS 125cc THRU 450cc UP TO 1968 (BOOK OF)
J.A.P. ENGINES 1927-1952 & MOTORCYCLES 1934-1952 (BOOK OF)
LAMBRETTA 1947-1957 ALL 125 & 150cc MODELS (BOOK OF)
LAMBRETTA 1957-1970 LI & TV MODELS (SECOND BOOK OF)
MATCHLESS 1931-1939 ALL MODELS 250cc THRU 990cc (BOOK OF)
MATCHLESS 1945-1956 350 & 500cc SINGLES (BOOK OF)
MATCHLESS 1955-1966 350 & 500cc SINGLES (BOOK OF)
NEW IMPERIAL ALL SV & OHV FROM 1935 ONWARDS (BOOK OF)
NORTON 1932-1939 PREWAR MODELS (BOOK OF)
NORTON 1932-1947 (BOOK OF)
NORTON 1938-1956 (BOOK OF)
NORTON 1955-1963 MODELS 19, 50 & ES2 (BOOK OF)
NORTON 1955-1965 DOMINATOR TWINS (BOOK OF)
NORTON 1957-1970 TWINS FACTORY WORKSHOP MANUAL
NSU PRIMA 1956-1964 ALL MODELS (BOOK OF)
NSU QUICKLY 1953-1963 ALL MODELS (BOOK OF)
PANTHER 1932-1958 LIGHTWEIGHT MODELS 250 & 350cc (BOOK OF)
PANTHER 1938-1966 HEAVYWEIGHT MODELS 600 & 650cc (BOOK OF)
RALEIGH MOPEDS 1960-1969 (BOOK OF)
RALEIGH MOTORCYCLES 1919-1933 (BOOK OF)
ROYAL ENFIELD 1934-1946 SINGLES & V TWINS (BOOK OF)
ROYAL ENFIELD 1937-1953 SINGLES & V TWINS (BOOK OF)
ROYAL ENFIELD 1946-1962 SINGLES (BOOK OF)
ROYAL ENFIELD 1958-1966 250cc & 350cc SINGLES (SECOND BOOK OF)
ROYAL ENFIELD 736cc INTERCEPTOR FACTORY WORKSHOP MANUAL
RUDGE 1933-1939 (BOOK OF)
SUNBEAM 1928-1939 (BOOK OF)
SUNBEAM 1946-1957 S7 & S8 (BOOK OF)
SUZUKI 50cc & 80cc UP TO 1966 (BOOK OF)
SUZUKI T10 1963-1967 FACTORY WORKSHOP MANUAL
SUZUKI T20 & T200 1965-1969 FACTORY WORKSHOP MANUAL
TRIUMPH 1935-1939 PREWAR MODELS (BOOK OF)
TRIUMPH 1935-1949 (BOOK OF)
TRIUMPH 1937-1951 (WORKSHOP MANUAL)
TRIUMPH 1945-1955 FACTORY WORKSHOP MANUAL
TRIUMPH 1945-1958 TWINS (BOOK OF)
TRIUMPH 1956-1969 TWINS (BOOK OF)
VELOCETTE 1925-1970 ALL SINGLES & TWINS (BOOK OF)
VESPA 1951-1961 (BOOK OF)
VESPA 1955-1963 125 & 150cc & GS MODELS (SECOND BOOK OF)
VESPA 1955-1968 GS & SS (BOOK OF)
VESPA 1963-1972 90, 125 & 150cc (THIRD BOOK OF)
VILLIERS ENGINE UP TO 1959 INC. 3 WHEELERS (BOOK OF)
VILLIERS ENGINE UP TO 1969 (BOOK OF)
VINCENT 1935-1955 (WORKSHOP MANUAL)

VELOCEPRESS TECHNICAL BOOKS – MOTORCYCLE

CATALOG OF BRITISH MOTORCYCLES (1951 MODELS)
INDIAN PONYBIKE, BOY RACER & PAPOOSE ILL PARTS LIST & SALES LIT
MOTORCYCLE ENGINEERING (P.E. Irving)
SPEED AND HOW TO OBTAIN IT (Motor Cycle Magazine UK)
TUNING FOR SPEED (P.E. Irving)

VELOCEPRESS MANUALS - THREE WHEELER'S

BSA THREE WHEELER (BOOK OF)
VINTAGE MORGAN THREE WHEELER (BOOK OF)

VELOCEPRESS MANUALS - AUTOMOBILE

ALFA ROMEO GIULIA WORKSHOP MANUAL 1300 TO 2000cc 1962-1975
ALFA ROMEO GIULIA TECH MANUAL CARBURETED CARS FROM 1962
ALFA ROMEO GIULIA TECH MANUAL FUEL INJECTED CARS FROM 1969
AUSTIN-HEALEY 6-CYLINDER WORKSHOP MANUAL
AUSTIN-HEALEY SPRITE & MG MIDGET WORKSHOP MANUAL 1958-1971
BMW 600 LIMOUSINE FACTORY WORKSHOP MANUAL
BMW 600 LIMOUSINE OWNERS HAND BOOK & SERVICE MANUAL
BMW 2000 & 2002 1966-1976 WORKSHOP MANUAL
BMW ISETTA FACTORY WORKSHOP MANUAL
CORVAIR 1960-1969 WORKSHOP MANUAL
CORVETTE V8 1955-1962 WORKSHOP MANUAL
FIAT 500 FACTORY WORKSHOP MANUAL 1957-1973
FIAT 600, 600D & MULTIPLA FACTORY WORKSHOP MANUAL 1955-1969
JAGUAR E-TYPE 3.8 & 4.2 SERIES 1 & 2 WORKSHOP MANUAL
JAGUAR MK 7, 8, 9 & XK120, 140, 150 WORKSHOP MANUAL 1948-1961
METROPOLITAN FACTORY WORKSHOP MANUAL
MGA & MGB OWNERS HANDBOOK & WORKSHOP MANUAL
MG MIDGET TC, TD, TF & TF1500 WORKSHOP MANUAL
PORSCHE 356 1948-1965 WORKSHOP MANUAL
PORSCHE 911 2.0, 2.2, 2.4 LITRE 1964-1973
PORSCHE 912 WORKSHOP MANUAL
TRIUMPH TR2, TR3, TR4 1953-1965 WORKSHOP MANUAL
VOLKSWAGEN TRANSPORTER, TRUCKS & WAGONS 1950-1979 WSM
VOLVO 1944-1968 ALL MODELS WORKSHOP MANUAL

VELOCEPRESS TECHNICAL BOOKS - AUTOMOBILE

FERRARI 250/GT SERVICE AND MAINTENANCE
FERRARI GUIDE TO PERFORMANCE
FERRARI OWNER'S HANDBOOK
FERRARI TUNING TIPS & MAINTENANCE TECHNIQUES
HOW TO BUILD A FIBERGLASS CAR
HOW TO BUILD A RACING CAR
HOW TO RESTORE THE MODEL 'A' FORD
MASERATI OWNER'S HANDBOOK
OBERT'S FIAT GUIDE
PERFORMANCE TUNING THE SUNBEAM TIGER
SOUPING THE VOLKSWAGEN
SOLEX CARBURETORS (EMPHASIS ON UK & EU AUTOMOBILES)
SU CARBURETORS (EMPHASIS ON UK AUTOMOBILES)
WEBER CARBURETORS (EMPHASIS ON ALFA & FIAT)

VELOCEPRESS BOOKS & GUIDES - AUTOMOBILE

ABARTH BUYERS GUIDE
COMPLETE CATALOG OF JAPANESE MOTOR VEHICLES
FERRARI 308 SERIES BUYER'S AND OWNER'S GUIDE
FERRARI BERLINETTA LUSSO
FERRARI BROCHURES AND SALES LITERATURE 1946-1967
FERRARI BROCHURES AND SALES LITERATURE 1968-1989
FERRARI OPP, MAINTENANCE & SERVICE H/BOOKS 1948-1963
FERRARI SERIAL NUMBERS PART I - ODD NUMBERS TO 21399
FERRARI SERIAL NUMBERS PART II - EVEN NUMBERS TO 21398
FERRARI SPYDER CALIFORNIA
HENRY'S FABULOUS MODEL "A" FORD
MASERATI BROCHURES AND SALES LITERATURE

VELOCEPRESS BOOKS – RACING

CARRERA PANAMERICANA - MEXICAN ROAD RACE (BOOK OF)
DIALED IN - THE JAN OPPERMAN STORY
IF HEMINGWAY HAD WRITTEN A RACING NOVEL
VEDA ORR'S NEW REVISED HOT ROD PICTORIAL

AUTOBOOKS WORKSHOP MANUALS & BROOKLANDS ROAD TEST PORTFOLIOS

FOR A COMPLETE LISTING OF THE AUTOBOOKS & BROOKLANDS TITLES THAT WE CURRENTLY HAVE AVAILABLE, PLEASE VISIT OUR WEBSITE.

For a detailed description of any of the titles listed above please visit our website at:
www.VelocePress.com

www.ingramcontent.com/pod-product-compliance
Lightning Source LLC
Chambersburg PA
CBHW070600170426
43201CB00012B/1888